Data Mining and Business Intelligence: A Guide to Productivity

Stephan Kudyba
Economic Consultant, USA

Richard Hoptroff
Consultant, The Netherlands

IDEA GROUP PUBLISHING
Hershey • London • Melbourne • Singapore

Aquisitions Editor:	Mehdi Khosrowpour
Managing Editor:	Jan Travers
Development Editor:	Michele Rossi
Copy Editor:	Amy Poole
Typesetter:	Tamara Gillis
Cover Design:	Deb Andree
Printed at:	Sheridan Books

Published in the United States of America by
Idea Group Publishing
701 E. Chocolate Avenue
Hershey PA 17033-1240
Tel: 717-533-8845
Fax: 717-533-8661
E-mail: cust@idea-group.com
Web site: http://www.idea-group.com

and in the United Kingdom by
Idea Group Publishing
3 Henrietta Street
Covent Garden
London WC2E 8LU
Tel: 44 20 7240 0856
Fax: 44 20 7379 3313
Web site: http://www.eurospan.co.uk

Library of Congress Cataloging-in-Publication Data

Kudyba, Stephan, 1963-
    Data mining and business intelligence : a guide to productivity / Stephan Kudyba, Richard Hoptroff.
        p. cm.
    Includes bibliographical references and index.
    ISBN 1-930708-03-3
    1. Business--Computer network resources. 2. Business--Data processing. 3. Office information systems. 4. Management information systems. 5. Electronic commerce. I. Hoptroff, Richard. II. Title.

HF5548.2 .K766 2001
658'.0563--dc21   00-054107

British Cataloguing in Publication Data
A Cataloguing in Publication record for this book is available from the British Library.

Data Mining and Business Intelligence: A Guide to Productivity

Table of Contents

Acknowledgments

The work is dedicated to my family, who taught me never to fear the pain and sacrifice of hard work in the pursuit of life's passions to achieve valued ambitions.

Preface

We are in the midst of a drastic transformation in the realm of commerce from that which prevailed over the past 50 years. Innovations in telecommunications, computer processing, and software technology have helped create the Information Economy. This term generally refers to the increased utilization of various forms of information technology (IT) to capture, store, extract, manipulate, analyze and communicate data and information of all forms by firms across industry sectors. As a result, organizations around the globe have greater accessibility to increased amounts of information than any time in the past. Because of the complementary nature of the IT spectrum mentioned above, firms can better transform vast amounts of data into a more vital asset, information, that ultimately enhances the knowledge level of individuals across functional areas of an organization.

As the information economy has evolved, the noteworthy progression of which began in the mid-1990s, economists, analysts and business leaders have devoted time and effort to identifying how the implementation of IT can increase the efficiency or productivity of a given enterprise. Many have referred to such innovations that have replaced factors of production in a direct sense, (e.g., labor displacing technology such as ATMs) as a primary driver of productivity growth. However, another source of corporate productivity comes in the form of "reducing the uncertainty of the business process." This idea refers to the process of accessing value added, firm-relevant information in a timely manner. The availability of accurate information enables decision makers across functional areas to better understand the important factors that impact the bottom line of their activities. A clearer picture of those factors enhances their ability to devise and implement policies that more accurately address the problems of a given process or augment successful processes to new levels.

The proper utilization of information technology therefore increases the overall "business intelligence" of a given organization. Enhanced business intelligence helps reduce the uncertainty of those issues that really affect day to day operations at the firm level. Keep in mind, however, that one of the pitfalls of the evolution of the information economy has been the proliferation of a variety of buzzwords and phrases that depict nothing more than a rehashing of commonly accepted practices. Does business intelligence fall into this category? The answer is no, for all one needs to do is analyze the growth, innovation and implementation of the spectrum of technologies that comprise this space to see the dynamic and tangible value added it provides to corresponding organizations. Firms of all sizes and industry types are utilizing these technologies to help augment their operations to compete, survive and thrive in this new dynamic economy.

Data Mining and Business Intelligence: A Guide to Productivity helps describe the process by which firms can increase their efficiency by implementing state-of-the-art IT. More specifically, it focuses on the high-end analytical software technologies, referred to as data mining, and how this technology, along with other applications such as On Line Analytical Processing (OLAP), can help decision makers extract information and knowledge from the vast amounts of data they collect on a day by day and minute by minute basis. This work is not written in a technical style but rather addresses the applied methodology behind properly implementing data mining techniques in the corporate environment. It provides an introduction to where the technology evolved (its theoretical base), an overview of the dominant methodologies that comprise the data mining spectrum and every day business applications where it can produce a value added. By doing so it bridges the gap between the important theoretical academic world and that of the applied side of the business environment. As was mentioned previously, we are undergoing a transformation in the world of commerce, which involves the evolution of e-commerce. This work has not ignored this growing phenomenon and addresses the issue of data mining in an e-commerce environment as well, connecting the more traditional "brick and mortar" firm structure to the growing "click and mortar" enterprise.

Chapter 1 provides the reader with an overall background of what the information economy and productivity at the firm level entails, which avoids a common problem that other works many times experience. Many works loosely refer to complex terminology such as the information age and productivity without providing an adequate description to ensure the audience's understanding of such principles. *Data Mining and Business Intelligence: A Guide to Productivity* not only connects IT to business but relates it to the theoretical underpinnings of where it originated. After providing the audience with this information, it then delves into a description of business intelligence and the technology that comprises this spectrum. The focus turns to a particular sector of the business intelligence spectrum, namely data mining, and offers an introduction to the various methodologies included in this "high-end" analytical area. Finally, it provides an understanding of how the various forms of complementary information technologies work together and with the addition of business strategy, can help increase productivity for a given business entity.

Once the reader has a general idea of what data mining, business intelligence and productivity are about, this work then provides a more in-depth description of the theoretical base behind some of the methodologies along with a more technical description of the main mining approaches. In order to illustrate the applicability of the various mining methodologies in a business environment some common examples are offered. At this point, the reader should have a good understanding of the concept of data mining, but to drive the issue home, we provide a definition of the technology and classify approaches according to corresponding functionality. At the end of Chapter 2, the reader should be better equipped to undertake the process of conducting a "high-end" analytical application. However, before one can take that step there is one more major requirement to consider.

As is the case with any new technology, individuals must learn the important steps to success for its proper implementation in order to achieve maximum benefit. Data mining technology is grounded in mathematics and statistics and generally requires a particular skill base in order to achieve appropriate results. Chapter 3 provides the steps to success and pitfalls to avoid when conducting a mining application. It then offers an introduction to a widely accepted productivity enhancing technique referred to as Six Sigma and illustrates parallels to data mining applications and the reduction of business uncertainty and operational variances.

In chapter 4 we begin to focus on using various mining techniques to help solve specific problems in the business environment. This section introduces such applications as time series forecasting and cross sectional analysis, methods which examine trends over time and over a "snap shot" in time. It provides some basic, non-mining approaches to time series forecasts and steps up to the more sophisticated methods, and offers common examples to fully illustrate the applicability of the technology. A more in-depth view of cross-sectional methods are addressed, which include examples involving B2B and CRM applications.

The following chapter focuses on econometric based mining which includes regression and neural network analysis. Since previous chapters of this book provided the background behind these techniques, Chapter 5 focuses more on some essential business applications which are common to organizations across industry sectors. These include in-depth illustrations of how the high-end data mining or information mining techniques can be used to measure advertising, marketing and promotional impacts on a firm's bottom line and provides important insights on pricing strategies. Finally, to illustrate the diverse applicability of these mining methods, we offer a number of common business scenarios in which these approaches can increase the users understanding of those factors that drive their process and help augment productivity.

Up to Chapter 6, this book concentrates more on the traditional "brick and mortar" structure of the firm. Chapter 6 bridges the gap to the evolving e-commerce "click and mortar" environment. The material in this chapter was contributed by an e-business organization (Engage Inc.), which provided some key insights on how to effectively utilize the Internet to help improve the performance of an organization. This chapter follows a logical progression from the previous chapter, which focused on advertising and marketing applications, as it highlights key issues on how to utilize data mining to more effectively devise marketing and advertising programs and better understand consumer behavior.

Chapter 7 then goes a step further by describing how such mining methodologies as Market Basket Analysis and related techniques, can be used to identify consumer preferences, which helps organizations focus on more accurately providing goods and services to individuals on a timely basis. The information in this chapter was contributed by another IT organization, Macromedia. At this stage, the reader has a better understanding of data mining and business intelligence; what it means and how it is used both in an e-commerce and non e-commerce environment. Chapter 8 then brings it all together by describing how organizations can utilize the entire business intelligence technological spectrum to reduce the uncertainty in particular business processes, which helps promote more efficient allocation of available resources.

In order to implement the BI spectrum effectively, one must not only know how to use the component technologies individually but must be able to integrate them properly. This can result in a number of obstacles that are difficult to overcome. Chapter 8 highlights some of the problems that exist in the implementation of data mining on an organizational level, one of which refers to a common issue involving the knowledge gap between "high-end" modelers and the non-mining community. It also stresses the importance of maintaining the BI strategic cycle. This refers to the procedure of identifying problems or areas of potential improvements, implementing appropriate policies to address these, and then monitoring the results of corresponding strategies to identify their success or failure, which then starts the cycle once again. The BI cycle incorporates all the components of the spectrum (data extraction and reporting, OLAP, mining and complementary Internet-related technologies) which help transform data into to usable information that describes the underpinnings of corresponding processes and enlightens decision makers to devise and implement more accurate strategies to improve process performance.

To sum up this work, the final chapter takes a look at what the future holds for the data mining spectrum. This is never any easy task, especially when considering the dynamic nature of the information economy. However, we have concluded that the primary source of innovation in data mining will not revolve around the development of new algorithms, but rather the wider application of existing technology and greater integration with such complementary technologies as the Internet and reporting tools.

Data Mining and Business Intelligence: A Guide to Productivity, seeks to provide a greater understanding of what various forms of information technology offer to the world of business in the evolving information economy. By connecting the technological functionality to prevailing underlying business applications, which incorporate traditional business and economic theory, we hope to illustrate the full potential of data mining and business intelligence in achieving increased efficiency for the firm.

Part I:

Laying the Groundwork
for
Data Mining
Technology

Chapter I

An Introduction to Information Technology and Business Intelligence

The world of commerce has undergone a transformation since the early 1990s, which has increasingly included the utilization of information technologies by firms across industry sectors in order to achieve greater productivity and profitability. In other words, through use of such technologies as mainframes, PCs, telecommunications, state-of-the-art software applications and the Internet, corporations seek to utilize productive resources in a way that augment the efficiency with which they provide the most appropriate mix of goods and services to their ultimate consumer. This process has provided the backbone to the evolution of the information economy which has included increased investment in information technology (IT), the demand for IT labor and the initiation of such new paradigms as e-commerce.

A DRIVING SOURCE OF PRODUCTIVITY: (IT, Economic Theory and Business Strategy)

Over the past six years, the US economy has been in a state of expansion which has included impressive growth in Gross Domestic Product (GDP), increased demand for labor and surprisingly low inflation. In fact, this lack of rising prices in the face of prolonged expansion has perplexed many analysts, economists and business leaders since traditional theory implies that as growth increases and unemployment declines, there is an increased probability of price pressures. One potential reason behind this anomaly of today's situation incorporates the notion of productivity at the firm level.

Productivity generally refers to the process by which firms use productive inputs to generate output. If they can more effectively or intelligently incorporate labor, machinery or technology and materials, they can better manage their underlying costs and maintain moderate prices for goods and services to the ultimate consumer. Firms can achieve increased productivity by combining the power of today's information technology with the tools of economic theory and business strategy. This notion has been supported by recent statistics.

> There is evidence that the US economy is in the early stages of a powerful new wave of innovation. The leading edge is the information revolution, which permeates every sector of the economy. Over the last year, for example, high tech has taken half a percentage point off of inflation and added almost a full point to growth...Since 1990, productivity of non-financial corporations has risen at a strong 2.1% rate, far above the 1.5% seen from 1973 to 1990. Manufacturing has done even better: Since 1990, factory productivity has been soaring at 3.6% annually, the fastest rate in the post-World War II era.[1]

Economic and business theory provide the fundamental underpinnings to firm level productivity as these disciplines address such issues regarding the utilization of optimal levels of resources (land, labor, capital and materials) in bringing a good or service to the market (Varian, 1996). Business strategy bridges off the more rigorous microeconomic theory by applying it within the corporate world. It addresses such issues as accurately identifying corresponding target markets, consumer preferences and effectively managing the process by which goods and services are produced and delivered to the consumer. Information technology enables corporate managers and decision makers to more effectively devise appropriate business strategy based on economic theory by facilitating the flow of information to decision makers and employees throughout an organization. Through effective use of IT, managers can more quickly analyze operations in the organization which include such areas as:

1) Production (inventory and process and supply chain management)
2) Marketing/advertising and optimal pricing
3) Customer relationship management applications (churn, response)
4) Distribution (wholesale, retail, e-commerce)
5) Finance
6) Human resources

7) Telecomm and network processes (call center effectiveness and network usage)

This notion of the enhancement of business efficiency through the use of IT has received increased attention from analysts and economists. In fact, Federal Reserve Chairman Alan Greenspan addressed this topic in his 1997 Humphrey Hawkins testimony to US Congress.

"A surge in capital investment in high tech equipment that began in early 1993 has since strengthened. Purchases of computer and telecommunications equipment have risen at…an astonishing rate of nearly 25 percent in real terms, reflecting the fall in the prices of this equipment. Presumably companies have come to perceive a significant increase in profit opportunities from exploiting the improved productivity of these new technologies.
What we may be observing in the current environment is a number of key technologies, some even mature, finally interacting to create significant new opportunities for value creation…Broad advancements in software have enabled us to capitalize on the prodigious gains in hardware capacity. The interaction of both of these has created the Internet.
An expected result of the widespread and effective application of information and other technologies would be a significant increase in productivity and reduction in business costs."[2]

Significant breakthroughs in computer processing capabilities (e.g., increases in speed and memory made possible by such processing from Pentium, AMD CYRX) have opened the door for a host of high powered, state-of-the-art software applications. Innovations in telecommunications technology, which has augmented the capabilities of the Internet, has further enabled the proliferation of vital information via intranets and extranets. The entire combination of the above technologies come together to create a vast information network that becomes the information pulse of a given enterprise. Essential components to such a system involves the following components:

Data warehouses	OLAP
Data marts	Data mining
Data extraction and storage technology	Internet-related technology for Web deployment (intranets and extranets)
Query and reporting software	

Of course all the above assumes essential core technology including server mainframes and the proliferation of personal computers to establish local and wide area networks and workstations.

For a more detailed application of economic theory and productivity refer to Appendix (1) at the end of this book.

AN INTRODUCTION TO BUSINESS INTELLIGENCE

The competitive forces prevailing in the world of commerce today require firms to operate as efficiently and productively as possible in order to maintain and enhance market share, profitability and shareholder value. An essential element to achieving success involves the continuous enhancement of knowledge and understanding of the business environment by employees at all levels. This is can be accomplished by implementing processes which augment the accessibility and communication of value added information throughout the organization. As a result there has been an increased demand for cutting-edge information technology by businesses in all industries. This increased demand has further resulted in an explosion in the development and implementation of technologies that store, retrieve, manipulate, report, analyze and communicate data. The increased availability of value-added information throughout the firm helps to augment the knowledge of the business to a variety of individuals. Decision makers can use information to better devise and implement business strategy based on Economic theory to more effectively manage available resources in order to best meet the needs of the ultimate consumer.

The BI Spectrum: Data Extraction & Report Writing, OLAP, Intranets, Extranets and the Internet

The above process has evolved into a philosophy referred to as "business intelligence." This topic is increasingly being adopted by management across industry sectors. Elaborate IT networks enable users to extract data (demographic and transactional) into structured reports, which can be distributed throughout an enterprise via intranets. As a result, information corresponding to particular functional areas is more readily available to consumers of the data.

For example sales managers can quickly view monthly sales activity by salesperson corresponding to particular products and in some cases the clients who have purchased. Of course, this seems like nothing new, however the true value-added of this process involves:

1) The speed at which reports are generated
2) The accuracy of the content
3) The degree of user friendly format
4) The ability to disperse the information to appropriate individuals

The next level of BI involves the organization of aggregate information that facilitates on-line analysis of corresponding business scenarios. OLAP or on-line analytical processing involves aggregating large volumes of data in a cube which can be accessed by information consumers in a user friendly manner. OLAP enables users to quickly view particular business applications:

1) Product/Service sales, cost and profits
2) Distribution information
3) Production processes (inventory, materials, parts and supplier information)
4) Advertising, marketing and promotion expenditures on products across regions of operations
5) Customer activities according to product or service.
6) Employee performance and activity rates
7) Financial details and many, many more.

By slicing, dicing and filtering on particular business application dimensions (e.g., cost of production according to a particular product line, corresponding to a production facility utilizing a particular supplier) "information consumers" can more accurately identify sources of successes or failures in particular processes and take appropriate action (e.g., apply a corresponding business strategy to enhance process efficiency). A very simple illustration of a cube is included below, but just think of it as a multi-dimensional viewing tool of various business attributes, where illustrations are both numeric and graphic and can be changed according to the users specifications in an on-line, timely manner.

Figure 1.1.

Time	Region	Product	Supplier	Parts	Measure
Years	Division	Product Lines	Names	Types	Cost
Quarters	Branch	Brands			Defect Rate
Months					Delay Rates

Basic OLAP analysis which enables users to quickly analyze the operations of functional areas of a given firm can help initiate efficiency enhancing strategies.

In the above case, this may entail switching to more reliable, cost effective suppliers, implementing new automation to the production process, (that reduce time and labor costs), or potentially outsource particular activities that can be done more cost effectively by outside partnerships. However the cycle does not end here. Business intelligence entails a constant routine of extracting corresponding information, creating and distributing accurate reports, and updating cubes for information consumers to analyze, identify successes and failures and take appropriate actions. It is only the continuous process of implementing policy and reviewing how those policies either successfully or ineffectively achieved the goals they were set out to attain which results in increased efficiency for the organization.

This brings us to the next level of business intelligence, which incorporates analytical technology that produces forecasts and identifies cause and effect relationships corresponding to a particular business scenario. At this level business intelligence involves the utilization of data mining technology.

BUSINESS INTELLIGENCE EXTENDED: AN INTRODUCTION TO DATA MINING

The term *data mining* has evolved over the years. In fact, as early as 5-10 years ago, many had referred to OLAP analysis as data mining. As the information age continued to evolve, which facilitated the availability of greater amounts of higher quality data, business analysts began to demand more information from this data. The proliferation of customized reports and the ability to scan data by geographic region, functional area and product or process performance, gave end-users a better picture of what was happening in their respective organization. In other words, complex information systems give information consumers or decision-makers a static view of their business. The next logical inquiry increasingly included such topics as:

1) Are there statistical relationships between variables in my data and are they reliable?
2) How strong are the relationships between variables?
3) If I change certain explanatory variables, what corresponding changes can I expect in the variable in question?
4) What can I expect in the future?

The term "variable" in these cases corresponds to factors that comprise a particular business application, (e.g., price, units sold, advertising spent…).

The term *data mining* today is characterized as the technology which incorporates the application of statistical techniques in conjunction with mathematical formulas that attempt to identify significant relationships between variables in historical data, which can then be used to forecast, perform sensitivity analysis, (e.g., what happens to my target/dependent variable when I change one or more of my explanatory/independent variables) or just identify significant relationships that exist in the data at hand. Some of the common methodologies that make up the world of data mining include:

1) Clustering
2) Segmentation and classification
3) Neural networks
4) Regression
5) Association analysis

A related topic that is often associated within the data mining spectrum is visualization. In this book we won't formally include this as a key mining technique but will classify it more as a mining augmentation methodology.

The following section will give a brief introduction on some typical business problems that require some of the more widely used data mining techniques.

An Introduction to Data Mining Methodologies

For the remainder of this book the terms:

1) **Explanatory, Driving, Descriptive, Independent variables** are used interchangeably and refer to those variables that explain the variation of a particular target variable.
2) **Target, Dependent variable** refers to a particular measure you seek to explain, (e.g., sales, units sold, defect rate, probability.)

Regression

One of the most widely used forms of high-end data mining refers to the application of regression analysis to historical data. This technique involves specifying a functional form that best describes the relationship between explanatory, driving or independent variables and the target or dependent variable the decision maker is looking to explain. Business analysts typically utilize regression to identify the quantitative relationships that exist between variables and enable them to forecast into the future. Some common questions that regression can answer involve:

1) What can I expect my sales or unit demand to be over the next six months given seasonal factors?
2) How does advertising expenditure affect market share over time or sales over time?
3) How does the strength of the economy affect my business over time?

Regression models also enable analysts to perform "what if" or sensitivity analysis. Some common examples include price elasticity, or in other words, how does a 1% increase in price affect my product demand. Other examples include how response rates change if I launch a particular marketing or promotional campaign, or how certain compensation policies affect employee performance and many more.

Regression also incorporates a probabilistic measurement between particular driving variables and whether an event will occur. Common examples, which involve the application of logit regression, include such topics as customer churning, employee retention and risk profiles. Given a sample of historical data, logit regression mining will enable the analyst to determine the probability that a customer will cancel, an employee will leave or how the risk profile of a portfolio will change in relation to changing the profile of a customer, employee or characteristic of a particular portfolio. The applicability of this technique is far reaching. The following is a list of a number of examples of how it may be deployed in business.

• Employee turnover
• Customer churn
• Customer response rate (mailing, marketing campaigns)
• Risk profiling (companies or individual's propensity to default)
• E-business Web site (effectiveness...hit rates)

Neural Networks

The next technological component of high-end data mining involves the incorporation of neural network architecture, which is also referred to as artificial intelligence, that utilize predictive algorithms. This technology has many similar characteristics to that of regression in that the application generally examines historical data, and utilizes a functional form that best equates explanatory variables and the target variable in a manner that minimizes the error between what the model had produced and what actually occurred in the past and then applies this function to future data. Neural networks are a bit more complex as they incorporate intensive program architectures in attempting to identify linear, non-linear and patterned relationships in historical data. This topic will be addressed in more detail later in this book, but keep in mind that this data mining approach can be used for the same type of applications as those mentioned for regression.

Segmentation

Another major group that comprises the world of data mining involves technology that identifies not only statistically significant relationships between explanatory and target variables, but determines noteworthy segments within variable categories that illustrate prevalent impacts on the target variable. In other words, segmentation technology that incorporates CART (Classification and Regression Trees) or CHAID (Chi-Squared Automatic Interaction Detection) will not only identify a statistical relationship between an individuals age and the potential to respond to a particular product offering, but will identify significant age segments that are more or less likely to respond.

For example, A credit card offering of free airline miles may be more successful with a particular age group and income level. Typical applications for segmentation and classification mining technology include many of those mentioned in the regression section and are as follows:

- Credit profiles
- Response profiles
- Customer/employee churn profiles
- Profitability, cost, revenue profiles
- Process (operational profiles)

The key differentiator between classification and segmentation with that of regression and neural network technology mentioned above is the inability of the former to perform sensitivity analysis or forecasting.

Clustering

Another major category in the data mining spectrum involves the application of clustering technology. This methodology facilitates the identification of relationships between groups of data within the vast amounts of information in a data warehouse. Through the incorporation of statistics and algorithms, the clustering technique seeks to partition large data bases into distinctly different groups comprised of variables that are statistically similar within the same group. At first glance, the user may mistakenly seek to apply a segmentation application mentioned earlier, however, this would be inappropriate. Clustering applications are designed to identify groupings of similar variables without the incorporation of a target while segmentation identifies relationships between independent/explanatory variables and a given target. The resulting groups or clusters help the end user make some sense out of vast amounts of data. For example, clustering may identify significant customer or product groupings.

One of the most popular clustering techniques incorporates the K-nearest neighbor approach which examines each new case of data to identify which group or neighbor it most closely resembles. The drawback of this application is that there is no guarantee that resulting clusters provide any value-added to the end user. Resulting clusters may just not make any sense with regards to the overall business environment. Because of limitations of this technique, (no predictive, "what if" or variable/target connection), this topic will not be addressed in great detail in the remainder of this work. For more details regarding this method and other mining approaches see Berry (2000).

Association Analysis

Another major component of data mining that will be addressed involves the application of association analysis. The association technique generally involves the process of measuring probabilities or propensities of the occurrence of a particular event given the occurrence of other events. One of the most popular association applications deals with market basket analysis, (e.g., what is the probability or percentage occurrence that a consumer purchases product A if they also buy product B). This technique incorporates the use of frequency and probability functions to estimate the percentage chance of occurrences. Business strategists can leverage off of market basket analysis by applying such techniques as cross-selling and up-selling. Association analysis empowers the end user to identify purchasing patterns of customers, which permits them to more accurately offer complimentary products or services to perspective buyers. This topic will be addressed in greater detail in the following chapter and chapter 7.

A more recent extension of association analysis has been the addition of sequence analysis to the association methodology. This is particularly applicable in e-business for Web site analysis. As the information economy continues to evolve, not only (.com) enterprises rely on the internet but the more traditional brick-and-mortar style organizations are adopting e-business by implementing Web deployment into the market place. Both (B2B) and (B2C) strategies are becoming common infrastructure in organizations throughout the world of commerce. Association and sequence technology analyzes (B2C) buy facilitating a type of market basket analysis through various levels of a Web site, (e.g., what does a customer click on and in what order, to finally reach the destination level of a particular site).

Association and sequence techniques are not the only mining applications that are applicable to e-business or Web Site analysis. Regression, neural networks, segmentation and clustering may all play a role in analyzing the vast amounts of Internet-related data. This subject will be addressed in later chapters.

Visualization Tools For Reporting and Monitoring: The Humble Chart

The final area in the data mining spectrum involves the implementation of visual aid methodologies to analyze patterns and relationships in your data. As was previously mentioned, this methodology is not grounded in statistics and mathematics but relies on graphic illustrations. Therefore, it not only plays a role in complementing data mining techniques but also provides a value added across the business intelligence spectrum (e.g., OLAP).

The graphical representation of complex data, often by no more than drawing a chart, is such a straightforward complement of data mining that it is often overlooked. It is extremely powerful because it provides a direct interface to the most powerful pattern finding mechanism in the world – your own eyes. The topic is covered in more depth in Neurath (1980), Tufte (1983), Zelazny (1996) and Horn (1998).

Application Areas

Graphical representations of data take a while to get used to. Typically, when you first look at a chart, a sequence of three things happen:
1. The patterns jump out at you.
2. You take a minute to find out what the axes represent.
3. You spend a few more minutes working out what the chart is saying.

The speed of the first step is the major advantage of visualization. The lack of speed in the next two steps are its main disadvantages. Visualization will therefore be most useful in applications such as reporting and monitoring, where the axes stay the same; only the numbers change. This eliminates the cumbersome steps 2 and 3.

Visualization is best applied for monitoring a regular stream of incoming data. Examples include financial market data and weekly/monthly corporate financial reports. In these situations, nothing will communicate the information more quickly than a chart, especially if the same chart format is used, day in, day out.

Basic Chart Types

A visualization should be kept as simple as possible. Axes should be labeled, units specified, and sources cited. Zelazny (1996) cites five basic chart types which people are familiar with and identifies the key types of patterns they attempt to convey. They include:

1) Pie charts
2) Bar charts (items, correlations, changes)
3) Column charts (distribution and time series)
4) Line chart (distribution *Figure 1.2.*
   and time series)
5) Scatter plots

The pie chart shows proportions: how a whole unit is divided up into components. For example, it is often used to show how big a slice of the market each competitor has, or how much each product line or region contributes to a company's

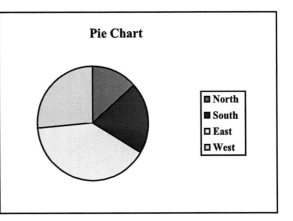

revenues or profits. Negative values cause problems for this chart.

Figure 1.3.

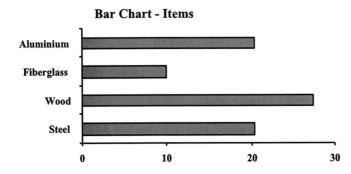

Simple bar charts are used to itemize quantities. Compound charts can be used to show correlations between variables or changes in variables over time.

Column charts, relying on the Western eye's tendency to see a flow from left to right, are useful for conveying quantities when the items being charted represent a logical sequence such as a time series or a frequency distribution.

Line charts serve the same purpose as column charts but are preferred if there are a large number of records or the records represent sample values of a continuously varying quantity.

Figure 1.4.

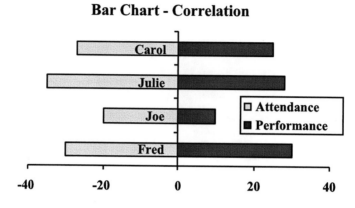

Bar Chart - Correlation

Figure 1.5.

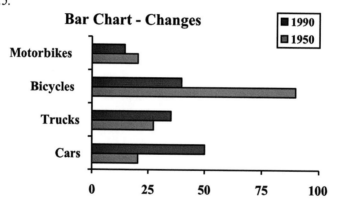

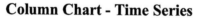

Bar Chart - Changes

Figure 1.6.

Column Chart - Time Series

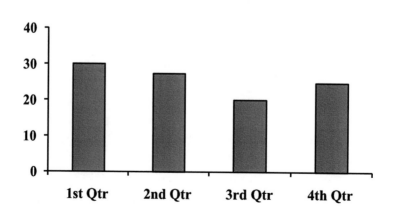

Figure 1.7.

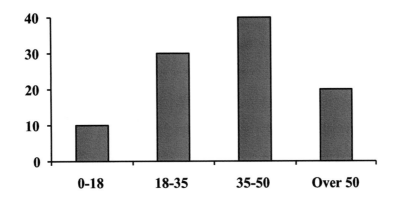

Column Chart - Distribution

Figure 1.8.

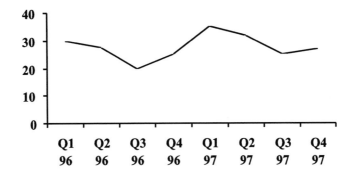

Line Chart - Time Series

Scatter charts are useful for showing correlations between variables when there are a large number of records.

In addition to the basic chart formats given above, an essential topic for effective visualization is a well-defined and logical color scheme. Color schemes of corresponding variables and segments of variables should be designed to highlight important relationships and not introduce meaningless distractions that may render the visualization useless.

Visualization can also be used to complement other mining methodologies. For example, association analysis mentioned above, helps identify the quantitative relationships between customer activities regarding product purchases. Approaches such as Market Basket Analysis help decision makers identify customer affinities. The addition of visualization to this process can result in a significant value-added to the analytical process by providing a

Figure 1.9.

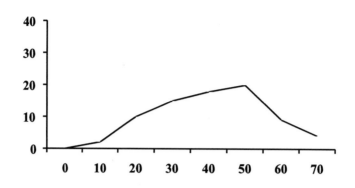

Line Chart - Distribution

Figure 1.10.

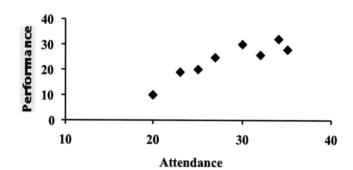

Scatter Chart - Correlation

Figure 1.11.

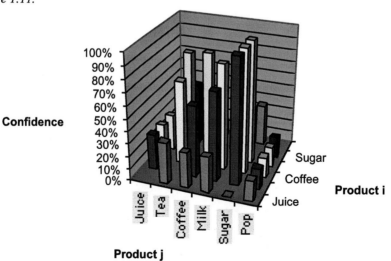

clear graphical view of existing relationships in the data. Figure 1.11 addresses this topic.

The analyst not only has the numeric indication of buying patterns but now can visually view the results. Within just a few minutes, the analysts can determine the likelihoods of purchasing patterns that were uncovered by MBA.

Visualization Tricks and Gimmicks

The complexities and gimmicks which are often added to visualization software can be a distraction rather than an advantage. Exotic or interactive graphical representations are, because they are new to the viewer, an unnecessary effort to interpret. The most effective visualizations are often created using the basic charting capabilities of a spreadsheet or slice and dice tool (with some effort to choose pleasing rather than distracting colors).

One gimmick which can be effective is the ability to animate a chart. If this is used to show the evolution of data over time, trends can be spotted through the eye's ability to follow movement very well.

Although visualization techniques are often taken for granted, the closer look offered over the past few pages reminds users of the true value added this methodology offers to various forms of analysis. As a result, many of today's data mining and OLAP offerings incorporate robust graphic capabilities.

This completes the introduction to business intelligence and the various mining methodologies. The next sections will more closely tie the process of augmenting business intelligence through the interaction and effective utilization of software applications.

THE BUSINESS INTELLIGENCE CYCLE

The components of information technology mentioned above all come together to comprise vast IT systems. Data storage, extraction and report writing technology helps users access and transform vast amounts of information located in data warehouses to a more user friendly format which creates business related reports in a timely fashion. As a result, the vast number of consumers of static reports within an organization receive information that corresponds to their functional areas in a more timely manner.

These software applications also enable users to manipulate granular level warehouse data into more manageable aggregated data that can be stored in a multidimensional cube. Once again, information consumers can readily analyze data according to business related subject areas. Effectively created cubes provide the environment for users to quickly slice and dice and filter on particular dimensions in order to conduct static analysis both in a numeric and graphic view.

OLAP users can more easily work interactively with large amounts of data through user-friendly navigation to increase their knowledge according to their corresponding domain, functional area or strategic business unit.

The mining portion of this knowledge enhancing process augments the static OLAP approach in a number of ways. One of these entails a reliability check in the cube building process. The effectiveness of OLAP relies on well designed and constructed cubes. Many times cube designers miss the focus of the information a particular cube should include or may include too much information. Clustering, segmentation and potential neural network mining techniques can provide a statistical value added to the cube building process. These techniques give the cube designer a reliable view of what types of variables relate to each other and should perhaps, be grouped together in a cube environment. Clustering provides the more basic approach to identifying statistical relationships between groups of data, which is appropriate in applications where data volumes are extreme or users have little idea of potential relationships between variables.

Segmentation gives a bit more detailed approach to the cube building process. Users who want to construct a particular business centric cube (profitability cube) can set a particular target and run numerous potential drivers through CART or CHAID to identify the significant drivers or variables associated with the target. This process helps filter out useless or noisy information.

Using Mining to Extend OLAP

The next issue in which data mining augments the knowledge building process is that it enables the decision maker to better understand the interactions between related variables that drive a particular business application. OLAP provides a tremendous base for enlightening users on what potential drivers are and have been. Mining provides the next step, which validates the relationships between drivers and also quantifies the relationships. It complements/augments OLAP by providing a more rigid examination of business attributes. Mining validates relationships through statistical techniques, which can yield more concise and reliable analysis.

Segmentation quickly provides a statistically based picture of the profile of your particular application. For example, does age or income level really influence customers purchasing habits and if so what are the significant segments that require further analysis? Regression and neural networks on the other hand, not only identify statistically significant relationships between variables in a given application but also provide a resulting model or functional form that enables the user to forecast into the future or quantitatively identify how changing one variable actually changes a target variable. A very common example refers to how pricing policies effect demand. Segmentation will identify whether there is a statistical relationship between the two variables and which segments of pricing policies affect demand but regression and neural networks enable the user to "plug in" various prices and examine resulting changes in demand. This process can be done over time as well to determine demand schedules into the future.

The power of mining is extended as it facilitates not only the identification of relationships between one variable and its target but incorporate multivariate approaches, which in many cases, more accurately depicts the essential elements of business applications. In the above example, demand is not only a function of price but incorporates such factors as advertising and promotions and competitors behaviors. Segmentation, regression and neural nets facilitate the analysis of multivariate business applications. For example, common business practice incorporates product differentiation strategies, which may include charging a higher price for a given product in conjunction with aggressive advertising campaigns to establish a differentiation from competitors. Therefore, a more accurate analysis is not just price on product demand but price policies along with advertising expenditure on product demand.

CLOSING THOUGHTS ON BUSINESS INTELLIGENCE AND PRODUCTIVITY

You've read about complex IT systems that incorporate data extraction, reporting, on line analytical processing, data mining and the communication of information within companies and between companies and their customers, partners and suppliers. These systems generally facilitate a more streamlined flow of data throughout the world of commerce. State of the art software applications enable information users to store, extract, manipulate, analyze and communicate greater amounts of data more easily. But what does this really mean?

With a more timely and streamlined flow of more accurate, business related information, decision makers across the pyramid of the structure of the firm, have a better idea of what is happening in the world in which they operate. Not only do they more quickly receive reports that are more understandable, but many can navigate through business related cubes of data to answer a multitude of business questions in a timely manner. At the higher end of this spectrum, they can actually utilize models that quantify relationships between business drivers, which enable them to achieve a more accurate understanding of what to expect in the future. In other words, if certain events occur or are proposed there is less uncertainty regarding the corresponding results. The key to business intelligence is the reduction of uncertainty in the business environment. The ability to capture, access, manipulate, analyze and communicate relevant data helps reduce the unknown. For example, decision makers have a greater intelligence regarding which products are selling the best in a particular region, by a particular branch, by a particular consumer segment, and can have a more accurate idea of what to expect in the future given the implementation of corresponding business strategy.

Reducing Uncertainty by Minimizing the Variance

OK the process sounds Nirvana like…however it isn't. The process of storing data and extracting the correct variables in the correct format corresponding to a particular business application is by no means an easy task, and has nowhere near been perfected. In fact, the entire process of analyzing information, implementing appropriate business strategies and monitoring the success of those strategies is a continuous loop of data storage, retrieval, reporting, analyzing and implementing appropriate strategies. This core decision stage of this loop entails analyzing the results of policies against what was expected, identifying the sources of variance and taking the appropriate steps to minimize those variances. Variances in this case refer to uncertainty in the business process, or in other words, factors that have influenced your policies, which the decision-makers did not account for. The reduction of variance simply refers to the reduction of uncertainties or unknowns in the business process. By reducing variances, management has achieved a greater knowledge of their environment and has greater control over the operations of their enterprise.

Results Don't Happen Automatically
(Technology must be utilized appropriately)

One pitfall that many organizations experience with regards to IT implementation and the resulting gains from business intelligence is that the link between technology and its effective utilization is not seamless, therefore enhanced business intelligence does not always occur. Appropriate systems, education/training and management skills are essential to achieving synergies from IT investment. (For a theoretical and empirical description see Weill, 1992).

Systems which can process appropriate volumes of data, which have natural integration both internally and with external partners and suppliers and are "user friendly" to the appropriate user are some core building blocks to an effective IT system. Once these fundamental issues have been achieved, which is not an easy process given differing needs according to functional areas within an enterprise, personnel must be trained or consultants utilized to achieve the full potential of the IT solution. Finally, and potentially of greatest importance, are effective management skills. Managerial skills require the know how to not only oversee the process just described (appropriate systems and user knowledge of them), they must be able to act on the information the systems are producing. Of course this process involves all tiers of management, from the lowest levels to the very top, from IT personnel to business strategists. Streamlining or optimizing this process should yield value added results. Investment in information technology alone does not insure firm-level productivity. IT must be used appropriately in order to extract the full benefits of its functionality. From data extraction and report writing, to OLAP and data mining, investment in education and training are essential to positive results.

Data mining involves the incorporation of more complex technology to help answer higher level enterprise problems, (how does advertising effect my market share?...how do pricing policies affect my demand?...what motivates my workers?). A requirement for effective data mining is the incorporation of accurate information with the appropriate methodology by individuals with the appropriate skills. The bottom line then is that with the proper IT infrastructure and worker skills to use them, business intelligence of the enterprise has a much greater chance to be enhanced. Decision makers can then ultimately apply the theoretical strategies of business and economics to enhance productivity and increase profitability and shareholder value.

ENDNOTES

[1] Mandel M. "You Ain't Seen Nothing Yet," *Business Week Magazine*, McGraw-Hill, Feb, 1999.
[2] Greenspan, Alan, Federal Reserve Board Humphrey Hawkins Testimony, July 1997.

REFERENCES

Berry Michael and Linoff Gordon (2000). Mastering Data Mining (The art and Science of Customer Relationship Management), Wiley Computer Publishing.

Gujarati, Damodar (1988). *Basic Econometrics* 2nd Edition, McGraw-Hill.

Horn, R. E. (1998). *Visual Language,* Macro VU Press, Bainbridge Island, WA.

Neurath, M. (1990). *International Picture Language,* Dept of Typography & Graphic Communication, University of Reading, UK.

Tufte, E R. (1983). *The Visual Display of Quantitative Information*, Graphics Press, Chesire CT.

Varian, Hal (1996). *Intermediate Microeconomics* Fourth Edition, NY: W. W. Norton & Company.

Weill, Peter (1992). The Relationship Between Investment in Information Technology and Firm Performance", *Information Systems Research,* December.

Zelanzy G. (1996). *Say it With Charts,* McGraw-Hill.

Chapter II

Data Mining Defined

Over the years, the term data mining has been connected to various types of analytical approaches. In fact, just a few years ago, let's say prior to 1995, many individuals in the software industry and business users as well, often referred to OLAP as a main component of data mining technology. More recently however, this term has taken on a new meaning and one which will most likely prevail for years to come. As we mentioned in the previous chapter, data mining technology encompasses such methodologies as clustering, classification and segmentation, association, neural networks and regression as the main players in this space. Other analytical processes which are related to mining, as defined in this work, include such methodologies as Linear Programming, Monte Carlo analysis and Bayesian methodologies. In fact, depending on who you ask, these techniques may actually be considered part of the data mining spectrum since they are grounded in mathematical techniques applied to historical data. The focus of this work however, revolves around the former more core approaches.

Regardless of the type of methodology, data mining has taken its roots from traditional analytical techniques. Enhancements in computer processing, (e.g., speed and processing power) has enabled a wider diffusion of more complex techniques to become more automated and user friendly and have evolved to the state of our current data mining.

THE ROOTS OF DATA MINING

The term *data mining* has become a loosely used reference to some well established analytical methodologies used to validate business and economic theory. The purpose of this chapter is to remind the user population that data mining is not some "black box" computational magic or crystal ball that provides flawless insights for decision makers but is an approach that is grounded in traditional analysis that can be used to gain a greater understanding of business processes.

Data mining incorporates analytical procedures grounded in traditional statistics, mathematics and business and economic theory. Much of mining methodology takes its roots from what is referred to as econometrics. Econometrics is an analytical methodology that involves the application of mathematics and quantitative methods to historical data in conjunction with traditional statistics with the focus of testing an established economic or business theory (for more details see Gujarati, 1988). The following phrase puts this issue in the proper context:

> "In reviewing the development of concepts for the statistical analysis of econometric models, it is very easy to forget that in the opening decades of this century a major issue was whether a statistical approach is appropriate for the analysis of economic phenomena. Fortunately, the recognition of the scientific value of sophisticated statistical methods in economics and business has buried this issue. To use statistics in a sophisticated way required much research on basic concepts of econometric modeling that we take for granted today."[1]

The evolution of modeling and mining dates back to the use of calculators in the processing of data to identify statistical relationships between variables. The estimation of such rudimentary measures as means, medians, max & mins, variances and standard deviations provided the building blocks to today's heavy duty computer processing of large volumes of data with mathematical equations, computer algorithms and corresponding statistical measures.

A Closer Look at the Mining Process (The Traditional Method)

The traditional methodology referred to as econometrics above involves the following procedure:

1) Gather data that includes information relevant to the theory to be tested.
2) Specify quantitative (mathematical functional forms) which depict the relationships between explanatory and target variables. (e.g., A single equation or system of equations).
3) Apply corresponding statistical tests to measure the robustness or correctness of the quantitative model in supporting the economic or business theory.

4) Optimize the quantitative model according to statistical results.
5) Draw conclusions from the procedure.

The above process relates to regression analysis, which was described earlier in this book. The methodology is used to identify statistically reliable relationships between explanatory and target variables.

Mining of Today

The more modern mining processes of today, described in the previous chapter, are dependent on a corresponding approach and incorporate relevant quantitative and statistical applications to produce a robust result. The level of statistical rigor and robustness of mining results depends on the application and mining technique. They range from lower level, basic investigation of large amounts of data (clustering) to higher end more detailed cause and effect identification between drivers and targets (neural networks or regression). The corresponding mathematical approaches and statistical tests fit the desired application. A brief but more technical description of corresponding methodologies along with a contemporary application is given below.

Clustering Revisited

One of the less rigorous mining methodologies refers to the clustering technique, which is often classified as undirected data mining. The term "undirected" refers to the fact that the analyst seeks to discover hidden relationships in the data without directing the analysis one way or another. In other words, the user does not specify a particular target to be explained (e.g., profit, revenue), but rather seeks to identify statistical groupings among variables. The approach combines computer algorithms and statistical measures to identify "clusters" of data or statistical relationships among variables. The methodology enables users to more quickly and accurately mine through volumes of information with a broad stroke of a brush.

In the k-means approach, the user simply chooses a k (or number of clusters) to be formed in the data. Descriptive fields corresponding to records are converted to numbers, and an average for the record is calculated which sets its location in space. The cluster is formed by associating those records closest to the original k seeds, set by the user. The process continues by regrouping the cluster seed according to its recalculated average of the corresponding cluster until the cluster boundaries no longer shift (Mirkin, 1996; Berry, 2000).

The traditional statistical measure to determine distances or differences between clusters involves taking the square root of the sum of the squares of

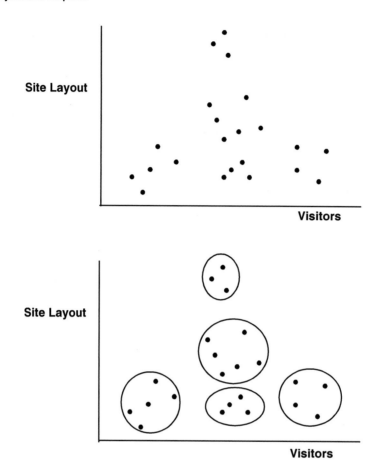

the displacements along the geometric space. The clustering technique often involves the selection of amount of clusters K by the user and displacement thresholds between clusters. The algorithm then performs the iterative process, which provides the end result according to input specification. The best result entails the smallest distance between elements of the same cluster and largest distance between differing clusters.

A more contemporary example of clustering involving an Internet application entails the following process.

1) The user selects a group of data, let's say, type of Web site layouts (e.g., product offerings, advertising), along with customer descriptive data (users).

2) The next step involves the determination of the best number of clusters (e.g., clusters with the greatest distance between them with the smallest distance between records in a cluster). The analyst can choose a number of clusters or some mining algorithms automatically identify the optimal amount.

The resulting analysis would identify the profile or group of customers that are associated with a particular type of Web site.

Association Analysis

As we described in the previous chapter, association analysis is used to estimate the probability of whether a person will purchase a product given that they own a particular product or group of products. Some basic underlying formulas which help determine customer purchasing probabilities include the following methodologies:

Market basket analysis looks at transactions to see which products get bought together. To do this, the transactions are analyzed to calculate:

N, the total number of orders.

n_i, the number of orders in which product i is bought.

x_{ij}, the number of orders in which both products i and j are bought.

Support S_{ij} measures the percentage of customers who buy both products i and j and is calculated as:

$$S_{ij} = \frac{x_{ij}}{N} \times 100\%$$

For a more detailed description of a basic methodology behind market basket analysis see Appendix (2) at the end of the book.

Confidence

Confidence $C_{i \rightarrow j}$ measures the percentage of buyers of product i who also buy product j and is calculated as:

$$C_{i \rightarrow j} = \frac{x_{ij}}{n_i} \times 100\%$$

Improvement

Improvement I_{ij} measures how much more likely product i buyers are to buy product j than customers in general:

$$I_{ij} = \frac{N \cdot x_{ij}}{n_i \cdot n_j}$$

With the use of these calculations, analysts can optimize customer marketing (cross-selling and up-selling) efforts in order to provide goods or services that more accurately satisfy consumer preferences. Market basket analysis and related methodologies will be addressed in greater detail in Chapter 7, which includes real time e-commerce applications.

SEGMENTATION AND CLASSIFICATION REVISITED

The next level up in data mining refers to segmentation and classification which incorporates decision tree algorithms. This approach is categorized as "directed data mining." Directed refers to the procedure by which users select a particular target that they wish to analyze, (profit, revenue, churn, activity rate). The user then selects the range of variables that may provide a statistically valid explanation of the variance of that target.

The most common algorithms that perform this procedure include Chaid (Chi Squared Automatic Interaction Detection) and CART (Classification and Regression Tree Technique). Without going into too much theoretical detail behind these approaches, the methodology generally incorporates the analytical procedure by which predictor variables are split into subgroups that impact or explain variation in the target variable. Predictor and subgroup classification as a reliable driver of the target variable are determined by traditional statistical hypothesis testing techniques including chi-squared and F-tests (Hawkins, 1982). Other statistical methodologies may be applied to safeguard against the acceptance of "borderline" predictor subgroups to maintain the overall reliability of the analysis. In other words, statistical thresholds may be incorporated in the methodology so as to filter out weak predictor variables or subgroups of predictor variables.

The resulting analysis should then potentially provide the user with a more detailed knowledge of cause and effect relationships between driving variables and the chosen target. The logical extension off of the clustering example given above would involve the following process.

The clustering analysis may have provided the user with the group of customers that were affiliated with a particular Web site. The next step could then involve a more detailed analysis such as analyzing the customer activity rate of a particular site.

1) Choose the activity rate as a target variable (click throughs)
2) Include the customer records and other Web site variables (e.g., type of advertising) as predictor variables to determine significant attributes driving activity rates.

The resulting analysis may provide the user with a tree view of the statistical impact of the driving variables and their subgroups (e.g., income and income ranges < $50,000, $50,000>$75,000, $75,000<$100,000) on activity rates. I use the terminology "the analysis *may* provide the user" because *sometimes there is no story in particular groups of data*. If the statistical tests do not render a variable significant as a driver in a model then the mining methodology will yield little value-added. If this is the case, the value added it provides for the user is the suggestion to search for new variables or data that may provide a robust story to tell. Some common business applications which incorporate the use of Segmentation are given below.

The most common approach to segmenting a database of records is the tree method. For example, consider a group of customers with the performance measure *Spending* (e.g., total amount spent in the last year). The group as a whole will have an average spending level, for example, 10.6. The group of all the customers will be represented by a box with this average value in it:

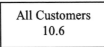

The process is to group the records according to one driving factor in such a way that the difference in the average of the performance measure is maximized. This is repeated for each of the driving factors. The driving factor is chosen which gives the biggest difference in average value of the performance measure between groups. For example, there may be the biggest difference in spending if the customers are grouped according to age:

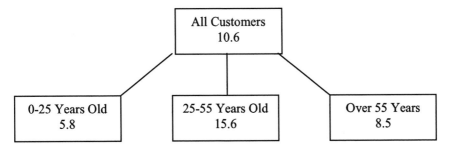

Note how the average spending in each group in the second row varies significantly. This process is repeated on the new subgroups until each group cannot be further subdivided with any statistical significance. For example, the youngest age group may not be further subdivided; the middle one may show a difference between males and females, while the highest age group might subdivide best by where they live.

The groups that cannot be further subdivided are the segments resulting from the analysis. In this example, there are five: 0-25 years old, 22-55 year old men, 22-55 year old women, over 55 year old Northerners and over 55 year old Southerners. This method of subdividing the records into groups shows the largest difference in performance measured between groups.

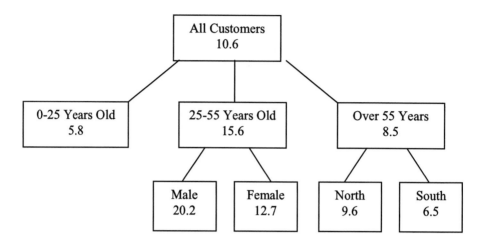

The process is limited by the extent to which statistically significant differences can be found in the data. This depends on the patterns in the data, but also on the number of records. Hundreds or thousands of records are usually needed for a successful analysis.

There are two basic ways to exploit the segmentation tool. The first is to use a tree to decide which customers to focus on. The second is to identify exceptional customers who do not fit well into their expected group.

Applications In Customer Focus

If the performance measure is chosen such that the preferred customers are at one end of the scale and the less attractive ones at the other, the segmentation tree provides a mechanism for identifying likely preferred customers according to their driving factors. This may then be applied:

- In marketing, to decide on which people are most likely to respond to a campaign.
- In sales, to identify which people are most likely to buy a product.

There is also some overlap with application areas more normally associated with regression methods. For example, segmentation performs well at employee retention analysis provided there are enough records.

A Typical Marketing Application

A typical application in marketing is direct mail targeting. A subset of the customers (the test group) is sent a piece of direct mail. Some respond, others do not. A performance measure is created in which respondents are scored

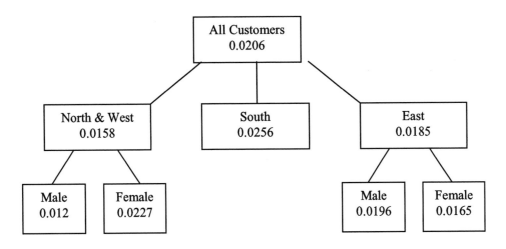

with a value '1' and the non-respondents are given a value '0'. The average value for the entire group is the response rate. The test group is then segmented according to demographic data about the customer. It may turn out that the most important factor is location, followed by sex.

The average response rate for the entire group is 0.0206 (2.06%). If I only send mail to the groups with the higher response rates (i.e. North & West Females, 2.27%, and Southerners 2.56%), the response rate will be higher and therefore the cost per response is reduced.

A Typical Sales Application

In a similar manner, a sales manager can work out which types of sales leads are likely to yield high revenues. A database is created which details all sales leads that come over a period. Driving factors are recorded for these leads. For example, in a business-to-business company, driving factors might include the nature of the request, the job title of potential customer, their industry and size of their company.

A record is also kept of the revenue that the sales lead eventually yielded. For leads that did not result in sales, a yield revenue of zero is recorded. This is the performance measure.

The segmentation tree in this application will then indicate the expected yield for a sales lead in a particular group. As further sales leads come in, the sales people can use the tree to assess the potential of the lead, and thus the energy with which it should be pursued.

Applications In Exception and Fraud Detection

A less widely applicable application of segmentation trees is in exception detection. Each subgroup identified by the segmentation algorithm will have not just an average value but also a distribution around this average. Any record in the group that is noticeably outside this distribution should be treated with suspicion. There are two main areas where this feature may be exploited:

- For highlighting potential data entry errors on a database.
- For identifying potentially fraudulent behavior in situations such as credit card purchases and insurance claims.

NEURAL NETWORK AND REGRESSION MINING (The Robust Approach)

The combination of mathematical/computer processing and statistical inference testing used to identify reliable relationships between explanatory and target variables comes to a head when considering the design of complex models used for "sensitivity or "what if" analysis and forecasting into the future. These methodologies also fall under the user directed category of mining and require the user to identify a particular target that is to be analyzed. These approaches also require the user to fine tune the selection process of potential explanatory variables.

Before we move on, it may be appropriate at this point to provide a bit more information on neural network technology which is also referred to as "artificial intelligence" since it has been growing in acceptance as a powerful mining tool.

A Brief History Of Neural Networks

The Perceptron

Dating back to the 1960s, neural networks were originally attempts to model the human brain. The first model, of a single neuron, was the Perceptron (Minsky, 1969). In the Perceptron, a weighted sum of the inputs was calculated to determine the output.

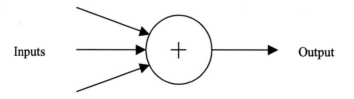

This could be used as a decision making system: if the output was greater than zero, the result was "positive", otherwise it was "negative". The weights were chosen such that the weighted sum determined which combination of inputs generated positive or negative outputs. The weight selection method (or "training algorithm" or "fitting method") was an adaptation of linear regression.

In essence, the Perceptron was a decision making system which used observations (data points in regression terms) to construct a decision surface (a line in regression terms). The fact that it could only fit linear surfaces had two drawbacks:

- nonlinear systems could not be modeled,
- no advantage could be gained by cascading Perceptrons (one linear mapping followed by another is still linear).

These drawbacks were acknowledged at the time, but no weight-prescription algorithm could be found for any system more complex than the perceptron.

The Multilayer Perceptron

At last, in 1986, the Multilayer Perceptron was proposed (Rumelhart 86) which used a cascade of neurons with nonlinear elements:

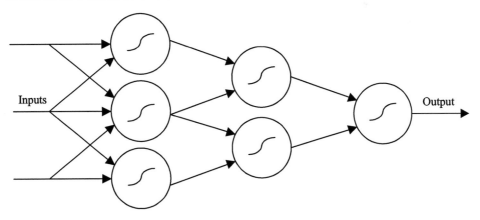

Each neuron takes the weighted sum of its inputs as before. This time, however, a nonlinear "squashing function" is applied to the result. This allows nonlinear calculations to be made. Any neuron can be connected to any other, with the restriction that the connections must pass from left to right, i.e. there are no feedback loops. Traditionally, the neurons are arranged in three layers which are fully connected to the previous layer.

While the Multilayer Perceptron was interesting to scientists studying the human brain, its greatest value was felt in the statistical community.

Ignoring the fact that it is based on neurons, the Multilayer Perceptron is simply a system for mapping from a series of inputs to one or more outputs in a nonlinear manner. The mapping is determined on the basis of a series of observations. To a statistician, this is a tool for multivariate nonlinear regression. In statistics and data mining, the neural network is simply treated as a method for fitting a curve to a set of data points. (i.e., The inputs are the driving factors and the output is the target performance measure.)

Avoiding Overfitting

The algorithm used to determine the desired weights is a simple optimization algorithm called back-propagation (Rumelhart, 1969). This is a simple steepest-descent downhill search. Although the optimization is local rather than global, few problems are encountered in practice. While other algorithms could be used, the steepest descent feature of back-propagation is attractive because it permits the use of an out-of-sample test to prevent overfitting (Hoptroff 92).

Other Neural Networks

Around the same time that the Multilayer Perceptron was developed, other neural networks were also proposed. These include the Hopfield Model (Hopfield, 1982) useful for associative memory, the Boltzmann Machine (Hinton, 1984), useful for global optimization, and the Self-Organising Map (Kohonen, 1988) useful pattern recognition. These have made less of a contribution to data mining, although Self-Organizing Maps are sometimes used for clustering.

Back to Regression and Neural Nets

The preceding provides the quantitative description of neural networks. Keep in mind that despite the complex nature of this technology, its functionality in the mining spectrum closely resembles that of traditional regression. The best way to compare the two methodologies is to state that traditional regression bases its model on a mathematical equation or system of equations while neural networks base their models on computer code. Both however, attempt to quantify relationships between explanatory variables and the target variable with the objective of achieving a minimized error in the difference between historical data and model projections.

Regression and neural networks may incorporate stringent statistical inference testing to measure, not only the validity of whether explanatory variables influence target variables, but also to identify potential relationships between explanatory variables in a multivariate analysis and the existence of patterns in residual terms. Residual terms generally refer to the difference between the estimates produced by the model and the actual historical data. Statistical tests can sometimes identify whether the given model that mines through the data is missing key variables that may better explain the variance in the target. This more robust or stringent statistical measurement sets these methodologies a stage above the clustering, segmentation and classification methodologies mentioned previously. The bottom line to neural networks and regression is that the resulting model that has mined through historical data can be used to forecast into the future or conduct a "what if" analysis given the addition of explanatory variables to the model. This assumes that the model is viewed as statistically credible (Wasserman, 1983).

For a definition of the following statistics see Appendix (3) of this book. Statistical techniques that are commonly used in conjunction with regression and neural network models include:

R^2 and Adjusted R^2

t- statistics

F- Statistics

Durbin-Watson Statistics

Beta Coefficients

Some neural network applications utilize statistical approaches similar to those mentioned above but differ slightly to address non-linear/pattern measurement between explanatory and target variables.

The above cited clustering and segmentation example can be extended to incorporate regression or neural network methodologies. To recap the process, clustering enabled the user to identify groups of customer profiles affiliated with a particular Web site. Segmentation and classification then identified the more important variables and sectors of variables that had significant influence on a given target variable (activity rate). Neural networks and regression could then be utilized to more clearly and reliably identify not only how explanatory variables impact activity rate but whether these variables influence each other and whether there are important variables missing from the equation that could better explain the variation of the customer activity rate. The resulting model would then enable the user to measure how new customer profiles would be expected to react to a given site. This book will offer more detailed applications using neural networks and regression in Chapters 3, 4, 5 and 6.

HOW MINING DIFFERS FROM THE TRADITIONAL APPROACH
(A Focus on Neural Nets and Regression)

Today's high-powered and automated mining processes differ to some degree from the more traditional approach described earlier in this chapter. The more traditional approach focuses more on testing an hypothesis (e.g., does price inversely affect quantity demanded) and involves the user in defining a quantitative/mathematical function that best describes or explains the relationship. The resulting statistical hypothesis tests render the functional form as either acceptable or unacceptable in describing the relevant theory. The modeling procedure often requires the analyst to test a variety of functional forms (mathematical equations) that best describes the relationships in the data according to statistical validation (Gurjarati, 1988).

Today's modeling or mining methods are a bit less intensive, as state-of-the-art technology automates the procedure. Many regression or neural network software applications enable the user to point and click to corresponding variables in historic data and let the technology tell them what is happening in the data. This is where the phrase "data mining" gets its roots. Analysts of today have more data to work with than any time in history. Data warehouses containing huge volumes of information are available for analysts to access to determine hidden relationships between variables. The higher-end approaches of regression and neural net technology today enables users to more quickly determine statistically valid, theoretical underpinnings in data unique to their business. The real difference between the more traditional approach and that of today's high-tech mining is best described by the paragraph.

> *Data mining is the process by which analysts apply technology to historical data (mining) to determine statistically reliable relationships between variables. Analysts use this procedure to let the data tell them what is happening in their business rather than test the validity of rigorous theory against samples of data.*

Of course, the process then introduces a subjective issue that involves the analysts interpretation of the results (e.g., do the results make sense to the business environment?). This issue will be addressed in the following chapter and in Chapter 8.

SUMMING UP THE DEFINITION
OF DATA MINING

At this juncture it is appropriate to offer a more formal definition of data mining before we progress to a more thorough description of the techniques, applications and general methodologies of the data mining process in the world of Business Intelligence.

As we mentioned earlier, there exist various mining methodologies that are appropriate for corresponding situations. In order to define data mining one must keep the definition in context of these various processes, which the phrase encompasses. *Generally, it is the procedure by which analysts utilize the tools of mathematics and statistical testing applied to business-relevant, historical data in order to identify relationships, patterns, or affiliations among variables or sections of variables in that data to gain greater insight into the underpinnings of the business process.*

One must keep in mind that the above definition is broad and encompasses the entire spectrum of data mining methodologies, but as you have seen, data mining techniques range in complexity and application. To clarify this, it may be appropriate to reclassify the high end category of data mining as "information mining" techniques. Neural networks, regression and to a lesser extent segmentation and classification, generally require a more focused format of historical data for a given analysis. In other words, analysts need to massage (format and transform) existing data in certain instances before applying "higher end" data mining techniques. As a result, users are analyzing information rather than just vast volumes of data. For example, information miners many times need to discover variations in (revenue, market share, credit rate, defect rate, churn rate or response rate), which can be a function of a host of drivers. Analysts must extract and convert corresponding data into specific formats which more closely depict business applications. The resulting data to be analyzed represent information that describes that process. This topic is addressed in greater detail in the following chapter.

The higher end methodologies are used to develop fine tuned business strategies through the use of sensitivity analysis and predictive modeling which differs from those techniques which merely attempt to uncover patterns and relationships in more generic and often voluminous data. One could consider directed data mining methodologies as part of the information mining spectrum.

This book will not formally address the different methodologies as generic data mining or information mining approaches so as not to confuse readers, however keep in mind that the term data mining encompasses methodologies which address different degrees of analysis. However, regardless of the degree of complexity, through effective implementation of data mining, users can identify relationships and patterns in data which increases their understanding of business processes and enhances their business intelligence in order to more quickly and effectively implement business policies to survive and thrive in today's highly competitive environment.

Before we go on to the next section, we will summarize the various mining methodologies in the following figure and provide a quick reference description of the mining spectrum.

A Broad Overview of Data Mining Technologies

The data mining technologies available today can be arranged according to their approaches and aims: *Just-in-Time Data* tools take advantage of technological muscle power in order to manage a company and its customers to a previously unattainable level of detail. The *Just-in-Time Data* methodology analyzes large amounts of data as it arrives at the organization. Conversely, *Strategic Insight* tools try to reduce this mass of data into a few key strategic insights. *Directed* tools set out to answer a particular question by identifying relationships between drivers and targets. By contrast, *Undirected* tools are unleashed on the data in the hope they can identify some hitherto unknown knowledge.

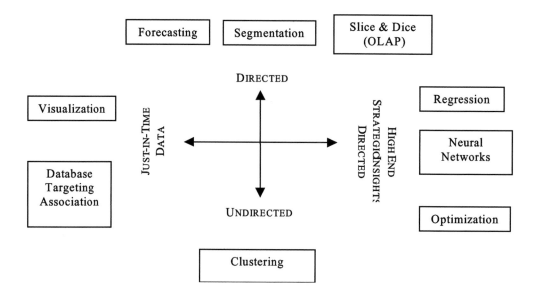

The main technologies offering value to business today are:

Association analysis. Association applications typically use customer behavior data to leverage cross-selling and up-selling opportunities. A typical example is Amazon.com's Web site. As each book is purchased, the customer is told "People who bought this book also bought..." (Amazon was invited to contribute to this book but declined, explaining that the issues were too strategic.)

Slice & dice. Slice and dice business intelligence tools allow a manager to extract summary level data for a business very quickly. For example, management accounts can be compiled for brass widgets in the Atlanta region for quarter one – on the fly, at the board meeting. Like database targeting, the power of these tools in not in their mathematical elegance but in the software innovations that allow the user access to the desired data in real-time.

Segmentation algorithms. These group data into segments according to a specific target. They are typically used to identify characteristics of specific aspects of the market (e.g., what characterizes my most profitable customers? Their age? Where they live? The magazines they read?)

Clustering algorithms. Like segmentation algorithms, these tools arrange the data into groups. The difference is that there is no specific aspect (such as profit in the example above). They group into clusters simply on the basis of similarity, (e.g., what basic customer types do I have? Should I advertise to each type individually)?

Regression and neural net tools. These tools plot out the data and try to fit a curve to it. The curve then represents a model of the dynamics of the business. Quantitative measurements can be taken from the curve in order to understand how different elements of the business impact each other: how advertising affects sales, or the impact of a price cut.

Optimization. Optimization methods are the most strategic data mining methods. Often they are so abstract that they do not go near the original data; they base their analysis on the insights gained from other data mining approaches. The other approaches deduce the true dynamics of the business environment. The optimization algorithm can then figure out what the best strategy is, given the environment. For example, a regression model can predict how customers and competitors might react if you change your price. An optimization algorithm can then figure out the best price to charge.

Visualization. Visualization is the graphical representation of data in such a way that a human can digest it easily. This is more than drawing a pretty chart. The aim is to communicate a large quantity of data to the human brain in a short time in order to take advantage of its massively-parallel pattern finding engine: the visual cortex. After all, why bother trying to build complex software when you've got something far superior between your eyes? Visualization is very effective for digesting a high-volume stream of regular data such as share prices or sales trends.

We've presented the theoretical background of the data mining spectrum and offered some basic applications in which each methodology could be used. However to get a real feel on what data mining is all about, we've included some feedback from a professional at a major corporation. The following section provides a true value-added to the material presented so far in this book as it brings many of the mining methodologies together.

At Disney we've used data mining extensively for market intelligence. It doesn't just benefit the bottom line, it makes for an easier life, too. It allows us to get our heads above the data and concentrate on strategic decision making.

Some of what we do is so simple you might not think it was data mining. Like charting our weekly viewing figures. It may not sound high-tech, but it is data visualization at its best: allowing us to digest a complex, regular flow of information quickly. By choosing chart views which highlight the key trends, I can immediately cut to the chase. Before the charts, I used to gaze blankly into a table of figures that looked just like last weeks' numbers.

The more exciting work we do in data mining is strategically important, so I can't give you the full details. We use clustering methods to understand our viewer's preferences in greater depth. This allows us to segment our viewers into different behavioral groups and come up with a programming schedule which puts the right shows on at the right time.

In segmentation, the value of data mining is to tell us which data about our viewers is relevant and which we could ignore. This is particularly important for a company like Disney, because our customer information isn't sitting in a database, ready to be used for free. We have to go out and get it through market research, and that costs money. Gathering data with no content is as wasteful as putting out shows that nobody watches. Data mining allows us to adapt our market research questions to get the maximum usable information from every research dollar we spend. In some advanced cases, the research questions even evolve in response to the results as they come in.

The ultimate example of the "faster, better, cheaper" effect of using data mining is in building customer behavior models. Advanced regression tools require less data than earlier methods and so immediately reduce the cost of research. They have the added benefit that they can kick out irrelevant correlations and coincidences, which are always a problem with research data. In our business, opportunities and markets constantly present themselves to us. Some will be profitable successes, others become languishing headaches. Early decisions about which markets to enter, and how, have a tremendous impact on the company further down the line. The intelligence we get from data mining offers a valuable insight, giving us the confidence to proceed with some choices, and making us pause to reconsider others.

— *Tim Julian (Disney)*

You've seen the theoretical underpinnings of data mining along with an authentic description of the process in the "real world". The following chapters will discuss some of these methodologies in greater detail as they are applied in today's economy.

ENDNOTES

[1] Zellner Arnold, "Statistical Analysis of Econometric Models", *Journal of the American Statistical Association*, September 1979.

REFERENCES

Berry Michael and Linoff Gordon (2000). Mastering Data mining (The art and Science of Customer Relationship Management), Wiley Computer Publishing.

Berson A., Smith S., Thearling K., Building Data mining Applications For CRM.

Gujarati, Damodar (1988). Basic Econometrics 2nd Edition, McGraw-Hill.

Hawkins, DM & Kass, GV. (1982). Automatic Interaction Detection in

Applied Multivariate Analysis, ed. DM Hawkins, Cambridge University Press, UK.

Hinton G E. (1984). *Bolzmann Machines: Constraint Satisfaction Networks that Learn,* Technical Report CMU-CS-84-119 Carnegie Mellon University, May.

Hopfield J J (1982). Neural Networks and Physical Systems with Emergent Collective Computational Capabilities, *Proceedings of the National Academy of Science,* Vol 79.

Kohonen T. (1988). Representation of Sensory Information in Self-Organizing Feature Maps and Relation of these Maps to Distributed Memory Networks, *Proceedings SPIE,* Vol 634.

Minsky M. (1969). *Perceptrons: An Introduction to Computational Geometry,* MIT Press, Cambridge, Mass.

Mirkin, Kluwer (1996). *Mathematical Classification and Clustering,* Academic Publishers, Dordrecth Holland.

Rumelhart D E, McClelland J L (eds) (1986). *Learning Internal Representations by Error Propagation,* MIT Press.

Shim K, Siegel G & Liew, C. (1994). *Strategic Business Forecasting,* Probus Publishing, Chicago.

Wasserman, P D. (1983). *Neural Computing-Theory and Practice,* Van Norstrand Reinhold, New York, NY.

Chapter III

Steps to Success for the Mining Process

The previous chapters have given you some background on the core components of corporate IT systems along with software technology that promotes "business intelligence" throughout an enterprise. This included a good foundation on the high end analytical portion of information systems, namely data mining technology. All this sounds fantastic, state-of-the-art software that helps increase the flow of value-added information which leads to a reduction of uncertainty in a given business environment. However, the bottom line to the productivity enhancing process from IT implementation really entails proper management and utilization of this technology. In other words, an organization can spend huge sums of dollars on the best systems available, but if they are not implemented properly, their value and dollars invested become useless.

Data mining technology is no exception. In fact, because of the more complex nature of the technology (e.g., statistics and mathematic underpinnings), the potential for underutilization or improper utilization is probably greater than other types of analytical applications. The following chapter provides some helpful hints on how to manage the mining process as it illustrates some common pitfalls that exist in conducting a high-end analysis. Remember, today's technology is good, but it doesn't do all the work for you.

MINING THE RIGHT DATA
(Garbage In, Garbage Out)

If this book teaches you anything about data mining, let it be this: If you gather your data poorly, you are destined to failure. No data mining technique or tweak can rescue you. If, on the other hand, you gather your data well, success will come so easily that you will wonder why everybody thinks data mining is so complicated.

The data you gather must:

- contain information,
- be relevant,
- be in a format which data mining can use effectively.

How Much Is My Existing Data Worth?

It is not uncommon to look to data mining to see if there is an opportunity to squeeze interesting nuggets of information out of an existing database. This is sometimes possible, sometimes not. If you are interested in visualization or slice and dice, your chances are good. If the database is in any way poorly designed for the task you wish to perform, you must accept that it will be easier to start gathering the right data from scratch. Avoid the temptation to mine a database simply to justify gathering the data in the first place: you will be throwing good money after bad.

A database is a heap of numbers, but that does not mean it necessarily contains useful information. Many of the numbers could be zero, for example, which would not be much use.

The first test for a database is to see whether it contains much information of any kind. Information theory studies this topic in depth using arguments which center around how predictable the data is. (See for example Price, 1980.) The conclusion of the theory is this: your database contains no more information than the smallest file you can compress it to. So, using a file compression routine such as PKZIP, try compressing the database. If it compresses to 100KB, it has ten times as much information as a file that compresses to 10KB, and so on.

The file compression test is a simple way of determining whether your database contains a lot of information. If it does not, you'll have to start gathering the data again.

In order to determine whether the information in the database is relevant, you will first need to decide what you want to do with the data. This book outlines some potential applications of data mining. As you go through the book, first ask whether the technique is applicable to your business. Then ask whether your database contains the data you will require. If it does not, you will have to start from scratch.

The final issue to consider when gathering data is whether the data has been gathered in a format which a data mining algorithm can use. Since the database was not designed with data mining in mind, it is unlikely to be in the correct form and some re-jigging will be necessary. For example, in order to do regression, it is necessary to roll up transaction data by month. Sometimes the data will be arranged in such a way that it is tantalizingly close to being usable for data mining, but not quite close enough. Often one vital piece of information which could have been gathered was omitted or discarded. Painful as the situation is, there is no point trying to mine this data. New data must be gathered.

THINK FIRST, MINE LATER: NINE EASY STEPS FOR SUCCESS

The database targeting, slice and dice (OLAP) analysis and visualization data mining methods generally present the existing facts to the user in a value-adding way. They do not try to interpret the data. It should be fairly clear what data need to be collected. The only real pitfall to look out for is errors in data acquisition – typing errors, misnaming columns, etc. A visual inspection of the raw data should be sufficient to spot any problems.

In the more core data mining approaches, the computer actually looks at the data and tries to interpret it. The computer lacks all common sense and will not know if the data being given are relevant and meaningful. Worse, it may not be evident from the computer's interpretations that the raw data is inappropriate. The remaining sections in this chapter describe the steps to follow and two pitfalls to look out for and discuss data gathering procedures for the interpretive data mining techniques.

Step One: Decide What You Want To Know

You won't get far with data mining unless you have a destination in mind. Buying a new piece of data mining software and trying it out on a database you happened to have lying around is not going to leave you very impressed with your purchase.

Data mining shows its value when it is applied to solving business problems. The business problem to be solved must be framed in terms of a question that can be quantifiably answered. For example, a marketer might not know the best advertising medium to use. A suitable question to ask would be: "How effective is television advertising over radio for my product?"

Step Two: Select The Relevant Performance Measure

(Users of clustering algorithms can skip this step.)

In order to make comparative judgements of good and bad, the relevant performance measure must be identified. It should be chosen such that the question being asked is seeking to understand what increases or decreases the performance measure. A suitable measure for the marketer's media spending would be Sales Revenue. Awareness might also work, although it lacks the same financial clout.

Most data mining algorithms require that the performance measure is a number. Naturally anything that is in dollars, inches etc., is fine. A qualitative judgement is acceptable, too, if it is expressed, say, on a scale of one to ten.

If you are measuring something with a yes / no outcome, such as whether someone responds to direct mail, it is possible to use '1' to represent 'yes' and '0' to represent no. The results you get from the data mining will then represent the probability of a 'yes' result.

Some mining methods allow categories, although it's often difficult to interpret the results. Avoid the temptation to label the distinct outcomes '1', '2', '3' and so on, because most data mining systems will assume that '2' lies midway between '1' and '3'.

Step Three: Decide What Each Instance of the Data Will Be

To look for patterns in the data, a mining algorithm will compare each of the different records in the database. Therefore the data you give it must contain directly comparable records, and there must be a healthy variation in the performance measure across these records.

In the example of the marketer, successive weeks might be comparable and then the performance measure *Sales Revenue* would imply sales during that week. If only a few months or weeks are available and sales are subject to strong seasonal variations, they will not be comparable, and it will be difficult to use weeks as records.

Similarly, each record could be a region. However, these vary in size. In order to make the regions directly comparable, a performance measure such as 'Sales Revenue per Capita' must be used instead of 'Sales Revenue'. This process is known as *normalizing* the data.

Many databases contain low-level transactional data; it will often be necessary to roll up individual transactions in order to obtain comparable records. In the above examples, the transactions have been rolled up according to weeks or regions. Rolling up the data will significantly reduce the number of records you use. This can be disheartening. If you find yourself mourning the low amount of that data, remind yourself that you are distilling quantity to make quality.

The number of rows required will vary between algorithms. Segmentation and clustering algorithms require hundreds or thousands of records to get a good result. As a rule of thumb, aim for at least a hundred records per driving factor. Regression and neural networks (curve fitting) algorithms require much less – the rule of thumb would be twenty records per driving factor. (In these calculations, if a factor is categorical, figure each category as a separate driving factor. Also, each category must occur at least twice.) If the records are months or weeks and seasonal variations are expected, you will need at least three years' worth of data to capture the seasonal variations.

Data Format

The following data require similar, comparable formats, (e.g., Advertising Spent and Revenue must correspond to the same monthly period). You can't compare weeks to months, months to quarters among variables in a model.

The following tables illustrate common data formats which depict historical data requirements.

Table 3.1. Not enough quarterly or monthly data to mine with regression or neural networks if there is a cyclical or seasonal influence on revenue.

Year	Driver Month	Driver Advertising Spent	Target Revenue
1999	Jan	$100,000	$1,500,000
1999	Feb	$120,000	$1,750,000
1999	Mar	$115,000	$1,800,000
1999	Apr	$105,000	$1,900,000
1999	May	$128,000	$1,800,000
1999	June	$100,000	$1,500,000
1999	July	$120,000	$1,750,000
1999	Aug	$115,000	$1,800,000
1999	Sep	$180,000	$2,225,000
1999	Oct	$105,000	$1,900,000
1999	Nov	$128,000	$1,800,000

Table 3.2. Enough data to produce a reliable model given seasonal influence.

Year	Driver Month	Driver Advertising Spent	Target Revenue
1997	Jan	$100,000	$1,200,000
1997	Feb	$110,000	$1,650,000
1997	Mar	$120,000	$1,500,000
1997	April	$175,000	$1,750,000
1998	Nov	$175,000	$1,500,000
1998	Dec	$210,000	$2,400,000
1999	Jan	$105,000	$1,200,000
1999	Feb	$115,000	$1,650,000
1999	Mar	$120,000	$1,500,000
1999	April	$165,000	$1,450,000
1999	May	$100,000	$1,600,000
1999	June	$120,000	$1,750,000
1999	July	$115,000	$1,870,000
1999	Aug	$180,000	$1,225,000
1999	Sep	$115,000	$1,900,000
1999	Oct	$128,000	$1,800,000
1999	Nov	$128,000	$1,950,000
1999	Dec	$195,000	$2,400,000

If you do not have enough data, you could:
- Get more data. If it is possible, this is the best solution.
- Change to a more sensitive data mining approach which can work with smaller quantities of data.
- Try a double roll-up (e.g., by region and by month). This will only work if there is genuine variation between the two dimensions. If Texas' sales are ten times Delaware's every month, you're adding redundant information.

If you are "blessed" with millions of suitable records, the data mining system may grind to a halt. There are three ways to tackle this:
- Sample the data. This is crude, but quick and effective.
- Roll up the data further. From weeks to months, for example.
- Break the analysis up into several smaller analyses. Why not do a separate analysis per region or demographic group?

For example, a (B2B) application involving data corresponding to supplier activity, for an entire fortune 500 organization may include several hundred thousand records. Instead of forcing this information through a corresponding algorithmic application (which may result in a time consuming process), the miner should consider designing a number of models from this data source. In other words, instead of creating a national account model, consider splitting up the application on a regional or product type basis. The corresponding data will be much less voluminous, and the resulting analysis most likely will yield more value-added results, (e.g., activity rates may be unique to a particular geographic region or product type). Tables 3.3 and 3.4 depict this situation.

Table 3.3. Organization-wide national activity model (too voluminous and encompassing)

Date	Supplier ID	Product Type	Location	Miles Distance/Dest.	(%) Delayed Ship
Jan-15	AADC	Parts	North East	20	2
Jan-18	AEDE	Materials	Mid West	50	5
Jan-22	BBCO	Assembled Comp.	South West	45	3
Jan-19	CCCD	Materials	South East	100	2
Jan-05	CCDD	Parts	North West	55	1
Jan-11	AADC	Assembled Comp.	North East	20	0
Jan-25	CCCD	Materials	Central	15	1
Jan-28	AADC	Parts	North West	55	5
Feb-02	BBCO	Materials	Mid West	145	3
Feb-01	AEDE	Assembled Comp.	South West	75	2

500,000 records

Table 3.4. A more micro-level model which captures uniqueness of client activity according to region.

Date	Supplier ID	Product Type	Location	Miles Distance/Dest.	(%) Delayed Ship
Jan-15	AADC	Parts	North East	35	1
Jan-18	AEDE	Materials	North East	50	5
Jan-22	BBCO	Assembled Comp.	North East	25	3
Jan-19	AADC	Materials	North East	100	0
Jan-05	BBCO	Parts	North East	75	1
Jan-15	AEDE	Assembled Comp.	North East	25	2

20,000 Records

The above model may provide a more value-added supply chain management analysis since supplier reliability may be unique to a particular region. Other filtering mechanisms could be product type instead of region. So instead of throwing your database at a particular mining methodology, the miner needs to take a step back and think about the problem he wants to solve.

Tables 3.1 through 3.4 depict two types of mining approaches, the former (3.1 and 3.2) with successive records over time such as weeks or months is referred to as a *time series analysis*; the latter (3.3 and 3.4) with a sample of records in a given time period is termed *cross-sectional analysis*. Most data mining systems can do both, although forecasting is usually restricted to time series analysis.

Step Four: Identify Driving Factors

The driving factors are the variables you think may have an impact on the performance measure. (In the case of clustering algorithms, they are variables that help to distinguish records.)

Some driving factors you may wish to include: In the example of the marketer, "television advertising spent" and "radio advertising spent" are necessary in order to measure the impact they have on sales revenue. Others will be necessary because they have a strong impact on the performance measure and therefore must be taken into account. For example, if the marketer's product had been discounted during the period in question, it would be necessary to include 'price' as a factor in order to account for its impact.

The limit to the number of driving factors you can include will vary according to the algorithm and the content of the data. At some point, additional factors will result in deterioration of the results. It is difficult to predict this in advance. Consequently, if there are many driving factors, try mining with a handful of the factors which, intuitively, you expect to have the biggest impact. If you get a reasonable model, you can try adding a few more, and so on.

Many data mining systems, particularly regression-based systems have problems if two or more factors are linearly dependent, (e.g., if you charted both it would not be possible to distinguish one from the other without looking at the axes). Typically, no result is obtainable if factors are linearly dependent, and unstable results are obtained if they are nearly linearly dependent. This problem is most likely to occur with databases with few records and many driving factors. Systems that suffer from this problem usually come armed with safeguards to warn you if a particular database is likely to be a problem.

Step Five: Acquire The Data

If some of the data isn't available:
- Try to find a surrogate variable – something which behaves in a similar manner.
- See how well you can get on without it
- Start collecting it so you can improve your analysis in the future

If one or two fields are missing some records, you have several options:
- Leave the field blank; most data mining algorithms have a policy for dealing with blank fields. (Often this is to ignore the entire record.)
- Insert the average value. The average value is neutral and so will not bias the result. Avoid inserting a zero; most algorithms will interpret the number literally, which is probably not what you want. (This is a particular temptation with fields for sales figures for product lines prior to their launch date.)
- If the data are a time series, you could interpolate or use the previous record's value.
- You can predict missing values of one driving factor on the basis of the others by building a regression model based on the remaining data.

Table 3.5. Dealing with missing data in a time series.

Year	Driver Month	Driver Advertising Spent	Target Revenue
1997	Jan	$100,000	$1,200,000
1997	Feb	$110,000	$1,650,000
1997	Mar	$120,000	$1,500,000
1997	April	$175,000	$1,750,000
1997	May	$100,000	$1,500,000
1997	**June**		**$1,750,000**
1997	July	$115,000	$1,800,000
1997	Aug	$180,000	$2,225,000
1997	Sep	$105,000	$1,900,000
1997	Oct	$128,000	$1,800,000
1997	Nov	$128,000	$1,800,000
1997	Dec	$190,000	$2,300,000
1998	Jan	$100,000	$1,500,000

1) For June add (May + July)/2 = $\underline{\frac{100,000 + 115,000}{2}}$ or

2) Insert May (100,000) for June. Do not input a "0" for June.

Step Six: Visually Inspect the Data

Create charts of all of the data and ask yourself if it looks right. Probably 5% to 10% of all factors aren't quite right, due to one error or another. Checking them now will avoid a lot of wasted work later. For example, in Figure 3.1, by simply viewing your sales data over time it is clear that there is a problem with September 1997. This could be a result of a bad data source, errors in data input or an anomalous occurrence. The miner has the option of correcting the data (if there is an error) or ignoring (omitting) it in the modeling process. If it is an error, the corresponding model will be unreliable.

Step Seven: Transform the Data
for the Most Informative Results

With experience, you may decide that using the raw data may not be as informative as transformations of it designed to give clearer results. Examples of such transformations include:
- Subtracting one date from another to calculate an elapsed period.
- Normalizing for inflation by dividing prices by a retail price index.
- Working with combinations of variables to spot specific effects (e.g., working with My Price/Competitor Price ratios rather than the raw prices in order to determine the competitive price elasticity).
- Working with market share data rather than raw sales figures in order to avoid seasonal variations.

Figure 3.1.

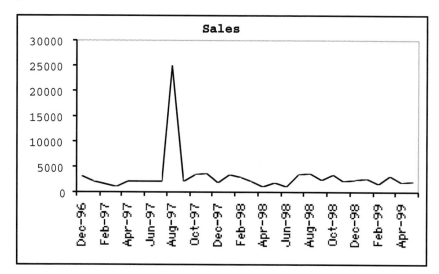

Step Eight: Mine The Data

Let the computer mine the data. This process is largely automated and it's a good idea to avoid trying to override what the computer chooses unless you really know what you are doing.

Step Nine: Review the Result

If the data mining system was able to find interesting patterns in the data, ask yourself whether they are plausible. If they are not, or no patterns were found:

- Ask yourself whether different data – or different transformations of the existing data – might give a more informative result.
- Do not attempt to modify the mining algorithm in order to get a better "fit" according to the system's goodness-of-fit measure. Many data mining systems allow you to override their well-chosen defaults in very unscientific ways. Most goodness-of-fit measures are quite simple and it is easy to outwit them by inadvertently bending the rules.
- If no pattern can be found, accept that it may not be there. Try charting the driving factors against the performance measure. If there is no hint in the chart of the pattern you were expecting, then it's probably not there. Ask yourself whether you are looking at the right data.

PITFALLS: TORTURING THE DATA TO GET THE ANSWER YOU WANT TO HEAR

Failure in data mining is not uncommon, and it is almost always due to the quality of the data that has been gathered, not the way the data mining process is applied.

Data mining systems are not temperamental mysteries needing great art and wisdom to master. They generally do not change their story much as their algorithms are fine-tuned. Equally, different algorithms and products from different data mining providers will tend to tell the same story. (If they didn't, would you have faith in any of them?)

It is very important not to fall into the trap of re-working the data mining algorithm until you get the result you're after. That's bad science. It may make you look good in the short term, but it will trip you up in the long run. If you're not getting the result you expected, you need to question the data.

- Might the result be the truth?
- Might the expected result be overridden by a more dominant factor that has not been taken into account?

- Might the data not be the best choice for testing your hypothesis?

Often a simple solution to testing whether the data is failing you is to plot it out on a chart. If you can't see some evidence of the expected result, ask yourself why. Very often you will conclude that you should use the data in a different way in order to get the result you need. Here are some typical real situations:

- A confectionery company wanted to relate advertising to sales. No impact was detected using data mining. A look at the data showed they were trying to relate this month's advertising spend to this month's sales. A time-lagged relationship would be expected. Last month's advertising turned out to have a much stronger impact on sales.
- A beverage company was trying to predict the impact of a price discount on sales. The data mining algorithm insisted that as the price was increased, sales would increase too. The data covered a 52-week period and the sales variation was dominated by seasonal variations. In particular, there was never any price reduction during peak periods such as Christmas and as a result the high volume of sales during Christmas season was affiliated with no price discount. To avoid the impact of seasonal effects, market share was used instead of raw sales. This gave much better results.
- A glass company could not see any pattern in their segmentation data. A visual inspection of the data showed several unexplained peaks in sales. Suddenly, one manager remembered that there were hailstorms in those months. The exceptional data (outliers or anomalies) were omitted and excellent results were obtained.

PITFALL: THE PURSUIT
OF STATISTICAL PERFECTION

It isn't just when you're not having any success that you need to question your data. You should also do so if your results are suspiciously good. Most data mining algorithms have statistical performance measures. If the measure is unusually high, you should question it.

For example, a management consulting company had a client who wished to forecast sales per square foot for potential sites for a new retail outlet. They built a system that predicted sales in the client's existing outlets with 98% accuracy. They couldn't work out why the forecasts for the potential new locations didn't look right, so they asked us to look over the model. It turned out that the clever data mining algorithm they had used was predicting sales per square foot by dividing one factor - revenue - by another - floor area. Clearly this gave an excellent model but is of no use to the client at all. (The fact that they didn't get a 100% accurate model with this data may say something about the value-adding capabilities of the management consultancy industry!) Since revenue for the new locations will not be known in advance, this factor had to be omitted. The new model was accurate to around 60%, which was much more in line with expectations. It gave realistic predictions for the performance of the new locations, and its explanations why were equally plausible.

The statistical measures used by data mining algorithms were designed by statisticians, not marketing people. As a result, a lot of the statistics sound low when, in fact, they're pretty good. This is most common when trying to find patterns in data in which there is a lot of random variation. In a recent case, a direct marketer wanted to throw out a segmentation model because the software was reporting a goodness-of-fit of 3%. The model was trying to predict whether each individual was going to respond to a mailing, based on some demographic data. The 3% figure was pretty good – demographic data accounted for 3% of response behavior; individual needs, moods and histories accounted for the other 97% of the variation. The model nevertheless had value. By using it to target certain demographic groups in the mailing, the response rate was doubled.

Finally, it is important to realize that statistical performance measures are useful for comparing the performance of two distinct but comparable data-bases which have been treated in exactly the same way. They must not be used to compare different approaches to analyze a single database. This is because many bad practices can be introduced which improve the statistical measure but reduce the value of the result. This is the statistical equivalent of surrounding yourself with yes-men. Good statistical performance measures are an indication that the data suit the method, not that the method is reliable.

A recent case highlights this point. In a pricing study, an analyst tried to build a basic model of the impact of price which gave a very poor fit. By going through the regression software and changing all the settings (actually by turning off all the safety features), a good fitting model was obtained. However, the results were counter-intuitive and very sensitive to small changes in the data. In this case, it should have been evident from the failure of the basic model that there was something wrong with the data. It turned out that the data set was only six months long – not long enough to account for seasonal variations in sales. The analyst should have been patient to wait for more data before doing this analysis.

BRIDGING THE STEPS TO SUCCESS TO 6 SIGMA APPLICATIONS
(Productivity Enhancing Strategies)

The preceding material in this chapter should not be taken lightly. In fact it should be benchmarked as a handy reference to those who wish to undertake high end data mining applications. As we stated in this section, there exists a host of data mining software technologies which are reliable in identifying patterns in data. However the most important factor to consider is getting the correct data in an acceptable format that helps answer a corresponding business problem. Referencing the steps to success should result in more reliable models that more accurately illustrate the driving forces behind corresponding operations.

Following the steps to success in creating a reliable model helps reduce the uncertainty regarding the underpinnings of business processes by enabling the analyst to identify and quantify the relationships between key drivers and performance measures. This notion ties in with a popular business strategy which is being implemented by firms across industry sectors. "Six-Sigma" involves the process by which firms seek to minimize variances in particular performance measures to fall within an acceptable output range.

More specifically, 6 Sigma refers to the notion of achieving a level of acceptable variance in a particular measure that lies in a range between (+/-3) standard deviations around a sample mean. Traditionally, this technique was used primarily for manufacturing processes where decision makers sought to achieve total quality management goals by minimizing the sample of defects in a particular production process. More recently however, managers have applied the 6 Sigma technique to a variety of business functions including such areas as marketing, services, human resources, finance and sales. Each of these functional areas have corresponding performance measures that need to be analyzed in order to reduce unacceptable variances. For example:

Reducing variances in production processes results in more efficient resource allocation. An excessive amount of defects (above average) may result in unfilled orders or backlogs in work in process cycles. On the other hand, much lower than expected defect rates (below average), which at first glance seems to be a positive factor, could result in over production and wasteful finished goods inventory levels or suboptimal utilization of resources once again. The essence of 6 Sigma lies in the minimization of variance that results in a reduction of uncertainty in a given process and yields greater efficiency in resource allocation. This variance analysis can be applied to achieving levels of customer satisfaction, employee performance and general process efficiency.

The key to achieving 6 Sigma entails identifying those factors that impact or drive a particular process and choosing an appropriate measure which represents the process output. The final stage is to gather data for the corresponding variables and conduct an analysis to build an understanding of the process and optimize the results. This procedure incorporates the Steps to Success addressed in this chapter and provides a link to high end data mining methodologies.

Regression and neural network models require analysts to choose driving and target variables that explain a business process. Once the appropriate data has been gathered, the mining methodologies enable analysts to determine the importance, if any, the driving variables have on a target measure. By doing this, analysts attain a greater understanding of what drives their business and, by applying sensitivity analysis, can better understand how performance measures change in response to changes in driving variables which in essence helps explain output variance. Just as 6 Sigma has been augmented to address a variety of applications outside of manufacturing, data mining techniques are increasingly being applied to a host of business related activities to help decision makers better understand their business which reduces uncertainty and leads to a more efficient utilization of available resources and increased productivity. The following chapters will provide more application specific mining techniques which could be used to help decision makers reduce the uncertainty in their business operations and help augment resource utilization to augment productivity. For more details on the 6 Sigma methodology see Appendix (4) at the end of this book.

REFERENCES

Pande, P., Neuman, R. and Cavanagh, R. (2000). *The Six Sigma Way*, McGraw-Hill, New York.

Price, R. J. (1980). *An Introduction to Information Theory: Symbols, Signals and Noise,* Dover Publications.

Chapter IV

Essential Mining Approaches to Problem Solving

Forecasting and "what if" mining generally incorporates the application of regression and neural network methodologies. In certain cases, for more simple applications, univariate forecasting methods can be used. Forecasting procedures are more affiliated with time series data or historic data that extend back in time (e.g., monthly periods over several years). Other mining applications involve examining a section of data over a specified time period, (e.g., looking at a number of customers, employees or processes over a given time period, let's say a six-month period). This approach is referred to as a cross-sectional analysis mentioned briefly in the last chapter.

The following section will describe these mining approaches in a bit more detail to give you an idea of not only how to effectively implement them, but also when and in what situation you may need to apply them.

FORECASTING TOOLS

Forecasting: Univariate and Multivariate

In data mining, the term forecasting means the prediction of future values on the basis of past values by means of a forecasting algorithm. In budgeting and planning, the same term has quite a different meaning and the two should not be confused.

There are two basic ways in which future values can be predicted from past values:

- *Univariate forecasting*, where a quantity such as sales is predicted purely on the basis of previous values of sales.

- *Multivariate forecasting*, where a quantity such as sales is predicted not only on the basis of previous values of itself, but also on other external factors.

Univariate Forecasting

Univariate forecasting is appropriate for forecasting a lot of quantities, where speed and automation are more important than forecasting accuracy. An example of this is to forecast demand for individual line items in a retail outlet or products for a manufacturer.

The basic principle is easy to illustrate graphically depicted in Figures 4.1 and 4. 2. Given a time-series of data:

Figure 4.1.

Look for patterns in the past to try to predict the future:

Figure 4.2.

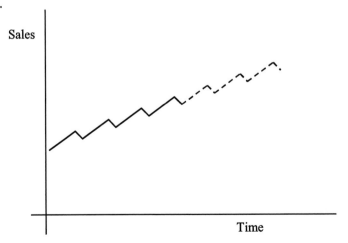

Clearly all such systems assume that trends and cycles observed in the past will continue into the future. There are a large number of forecasting algorithms available (Makridakis, 1983), but in practice, choice of forecasting algorithm is not very important. With certain data, one algorithm may have a marginal advantage over another. However, in an automated system with real data, they tend to yield similar results; the forecasting accuracy is dominated by the degree to which the data has clear trends and cycles rather than the choice of algorithm.

Most univariate forecasting systems require two years' worth of data in order to capture both seasonal patterns and longer term growth trends.

Implementing a Simple
Univariate Forecasting System

Univariate forecasting systems are often available from database suppliers. If not, a simple system which performs moderately well, and has the advantage of being simple and therefore robust, is as follows:

1. To capture the trend, take the last two years of data and total them up individually to estimate the annual year-on-year growth figure.
2. Predict future years' growth by the annual growth values to the most recent year's total.
3. Break down the annual forecasts by sharing them in proportionately according to the sales in the most recent year.

Table 4.1. provides an example:

Date	Original Data	Step 1: Annual totals	Step 2: Apply Growth Rate	Step 3: Apportion Quarters	Final Forecast
Q1 1998	2				2
Q2 1998	5				5
Q3 1998	6	16	16		6
Q4 1998	3				3
Q1 1999	3				3
Q2 1999	8				8
Q3 1999	9	25	25		9
Q4 1999	5				5
Q1 2000				$39 \leftrightarrow \frac{3}{25} = 4.7$	4.7
Q2 2000			$25 \leftrightarrow \frac{25}{16} = 39$	$39 \leftrightarrow \frac{8}{25} = 12.5$	12.5
Q3 2000				$39 \leftrightarrow \frac{9}{25} = 14.0$	14.0
Q4 2000				$39 \leftrightarrow \frac{5}{25} = 7.8$	7.8
Q1 2001				$61 \leftrightarrow \frac{3}{25} = 7.3$	7.3
Q2 2001			$39 \leftrightarrow \frac{25}{16} = 61$	$61 \leftrightarrow \frac{8}{25} = 19.5$	19.5
Q3 2001				$61 \leftrightarrow \frac{9}{25} = 22.0$	22.0
Q4 2001				$61 \leftrightarrow \frac{5}{25} = 12.2$	12.2

Univariate forecasting can incorporate a variety of mathematical approaches that analyze past data in the attempt to forecast the future. The prevalent methodologies include: moving averages, exponential smoothing and applying linear weights (Shim, 1994) and are illustrated in Table 4.2.

Univariate Forecasting with Regression and Neural Networks

To implement univariate forecasting in a regression or neural network system, the quantity you wish to forecast is used as the target measure. One driving factor is used to capture the trend. This should be a steadily increasing number or one that increases incrementally annually. (It is usual to use the year as a number, e.g., 1999). The other driving factor should be a categoric variable, with one value per seasonal unit, e.g., Jan., Feb., etc., which repeats itself each year.

The forecasts are obtained by applying future values, e.g., 2003, Jan. to the model and observing the predicted value for the target measure.

The cross sections are of limited value in a univariate forecast. They show the underlying growth trend and seasonal pattern respectively, but offer no explanation as to why these patterns exist.

Table 4.2 depicts a basic data format for forecasting a number of items (e.g., products, product lines, branches, subsidiaries, regions) along with some examples of univariate forecasting approaches.

Table 4.2.

Year	Month	Product (a)	Product (b)	Product (c)	Product (d)
1999	Jan	100,000	500,000	750,000	450,000
1999	Feb	120,000	750,000	300,000	250,000
1999	Mar	115,000	800,000	225,000	200,000
1999	Apr	105,000	900,000	450,000	400,000
1999	May	128,000	800,000	345,000	460,000
1999	June	100,000	500,000	560,000	600,000
1999	July	120,000	750,000	700,000	670,000

bivariate examples:
1) 4 Month moving average Poduct (a):

$$\frac{105,000 + 128,000 + 100,000 + 120,000}{4} = \text{August's expected demand}$$

2) Exponential Smooth for Poduct (a):
Equation (YH) =   α(Y) + (1-a)(Y-1)
(.75 x 120,000) + (.25 x 100,000) = August's expected demand

To Recap:

Univariate forecasting techniques can be used as above, which incorporate the prediction of future demand for the corresponding product lines from calculations of past demand data.

Univariate forecasting with regression and neural networks incorporate time (year) and season (months) in identifying seasonal/cyclical patterns from past data to forecast into the future. Both methodologies require a minimum of two years of historical data to produce reliable results.

Multivariate Forecasting

Multivariate forecasts predict a data series using factors other than previous values of the quantity being forecast. This will generate a more accurate forecast but will require more thought and interaction with the forecasting system. The extra effort is worth it in complex, high-level forecasting models, where many effects need to be considered (Hoptroff, 1992). It also allows forecasts to be made for a variety of scenarios.

The basic principle can be demonstrated in a manner similar to univariate forecasting. Given a target measure such as sales, and a driving factor such as price:

Figure 4.3.

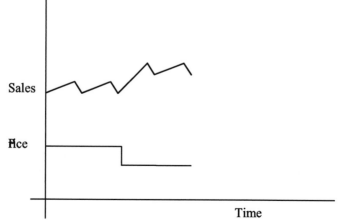

A clear pattern between the two is evident. A regression or neural net system quantifies this pattern to predict sales in the future:

Figure 4.4.

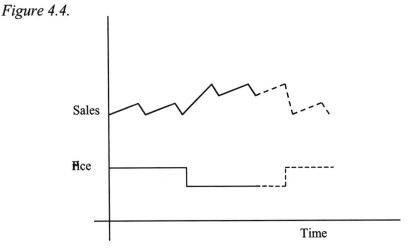

Note that it was necessary to extend the driving factor into the future in order to predict sales in the future. There are three ways to do this, and two ways to avoid it:

- If the driving factor is well-behaved, it can be predicted using univariate forecasting.
- If the driving factor is, in turn, driven by another factor (e.g., a competitor's price might always be in close proximity to yours), this relationship can be modeled as a separate regression exercise.
- If the variable is under the user's control, (such as price in this case), future planned values can be fed directly into the system.
- If past values of the driving factor might plausibly be responsible for future changes in the performance measure, the driving variable can be lagged. For example, if last month's value of advertising is used to predict this month's value of sales, it would be possible to predict next month's sales using data available today.
- If the variable is very difficult to predict, the user can try different values in order to come up with best case'and worst case'scenarios.

Multivariate forecasts obtained using regression or neural networks require the same skills and tools as for other applications, although it is clearly useful to have features to extrapolate past values out into the future.

In multivariate forecasting, it is often useful to include seasonal driving factors (e.g., Jan., Feb., etc.) if there are seasonal variations in demand that would be difficult to express to the system in any other way. The trend-driving factor (i.e., the year number, 1999, 2000, etc.) is usually omitted because the aim is usually to encourage the other driving factors to explain the trends, not an arbitrary trend variable. Including the trend variable also makes the cross-sections more difficult to interpret.

The data format depicted in Table 4.3 refers to a simple multivariate application for regression or neural networks. Generally, it incorporates a more thorough analysis of forecasting for Product (a) in the univariate approach depicted in Table 4.2. This application incorporates seasons (month) and price as explanatory variables of Product (a)'s unit demand. Other explanatory variables could include advertising or marketing expenditures.

Table 4.3.

Year	Month	Price	Product (a)
1999	Jan	210	100,000
1999	Feb	200	120,000
1999	Mar	200	115,000
1999	Apr	180	180,000
1999	May	220	105,000
1999	Jun	215	128,000

To recap, forecasting techniques are not cookie-cutter solution applications. The proper technique (e.g., univariate or multivariate) is dependent on the solution at hand. This requires the miner to understand the business in which they are operating and the question to be answered. Forecasting demands of numerous product lines or revenue of corporate branches where data is highly cyclical may only require a univariate or seasonality approach. Applications such as advertising effectiveness or product demand for a particular unique product (e.g., differentiated product) or revenue for an entire organization may require such independent variables as price, promotions, macroeconomic growth indicators, marketing and more. True value-added mining requires not only appropriate methodologies and reliable technology but the user ability to know what to include in a given analysis.

FROM ANALYSIS OVER TIME
TO ANALYSIS OF A SNAPSHOT IN TIME

Mining methodologies also are applicable to a particular sample of data over a specific point in time. For example, marketing analysts may be interested in how a particular mailing campaign had fared or the effectiveness of a particular Web site. Manufacturing quality control analysts may be interested in how particular processes perform or researchers may be interested in survey results. Instead of looking at the results of a particular strategy over time, analysts may be interested in how a variety of campaigns or processes perform. This methodology refers to a cross-sectional analysis briefly mentioned in the last chapter.

To better illustrate this topic, consider a basic survey. Marketing research analysts most likely will not be interested in how a particular individual responded to various surveys over the past few years and most likely don't have that kind of data anyway. Instead, they have a snapshot of how a number of individuals with specific characteristics responded to a particular survey over a particular period, let's say the questionnaire was launched over a period of three months. The corresponding input data (Table 4.4), will differ from the time series approach mentioned previously. For example:

Table 4.4.

Name	Age	Gender	Income	Residence	Marital Status	Response Measure
ABC	24	M	50K	City	Single	100
DEA	30	M	40K	City	Single	90
CDR	24	M	50K	City	Single	98
RNB	30	F	45K	Suburban	Married	85
DGH	34	M	30K	City	Married	70
WCH	25	F	40K	Rural	Single	90
UTY	36	M	48K	City	Married	65
DSF	25	M	35K	City	Single	110
GIH	38	F	60K	Suburban	Married	55

As you can see, there is a difference from a time series analysis, as the data format includes a sample of responses. From this, analysts can determine if there are any significant patterns among descriptive variables of particular respondents. Mining methodologies such as regression, neural networks or segmentation and classification rules are well suited to analyze this data. These methodologies generally measure the repeated frequency of similar respondents to quantify a likelihood of response. Other examples include applications analyzing production processes which may involve row by row data that includes plant location, units produced, supplier of parts, type of parts, and machine hours used, where the corresponding measure may be a defect rate.

Figure 4.5.

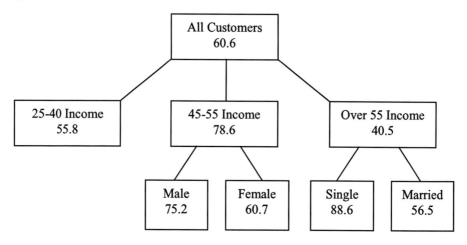

Segmentation and classification methodologies will identify statistically significant relationships between the explanatory or driving variables along with significant segments within a variable (e.g., not only income but income segments that are associated with particular response rates in the data above) and the target measure. The user can then identify which segments of a particular variable drive the highest or lowest response rates which is depicted in Figure 4.5.

In order to target the profile of people responding with the highest survey rate the analyst would focus on men in the income range between $45,000 and $55,000.

Regression and neural network methodologies will do much of the same but will not separate distinct segment breaks within a variable. These methodologies will identify an overall relationship between the entire variable and the corresponding target measure. These models also enable the user to perform "what if" analysis and actually score a new sample of customer data. For example in a (0/1), (Yes/No) response application described in the next section, regression or neural net models rank individual response rates on an existing sample of cross-sectional data. The models can then be applied to new data to generate probability or activity scores of these individuals.

This process enables users to more accurately apply business strategies such as the widely cited "80/20" rule by scoring individuals. With the use of these mining methodologies, analysts can identify those individuals that are more likely to respond and focus mailing campaigns accordingly. Therefore, the campaign population can be cut down drastically while maintaining the same response rate. The result of this process should yield increased productivity for the corresponding firm from a more effective allocation of resources. In other words, by more accurately identifying target markets, firms can reduce wasted ineffective resource allocation (e.g., costs associated with marketing, advertising activities which include labor, capital and materials).

Target Measures and Probability Mining

When implementing a cross-sectional mining approach, the target measure can be defined in different ways. For example, in a customer churn application, analysts may want to identify the types of customers that account for the amount of most lost business.

The target variable would then be defined as some measure of lost business. One way to do this is to calculate the dollar amount of business customers had done with your company (e.g., transaction amount, products purchased) and use this as the target measure. With this application, the user not only identifies the type of customer that is leaving but the rank of that customer according to value to your business.

Other target variables include such measures as:

1) Defect Rate (Process analysis)
2) Default Rate (Credit analysis)
3) Rankings (Survey results e.g., 1 – 10)
4) Response or Churn Rate (0/1) for Yes or No
5) Basic measures (e.g., value of lost business mentioned above)

Many of these targets, especially number (4) Response or Churn Rate incorporate the methodology of probability measurement. The formal mining methodology is referred to as Logit Regression; however, neural networks are also capable of calculating this type of analysis. Logit Regression is a generalization of linear regression and is used for modeling with a binary (0/1) target. This methodology helps determine the probability, odds or likelihood that an event will occur, (e.g., a customer will respond, an employee will leave or a client will click through a Web site) based on past behavior. This technique is often referred to as profiling where resulting regression or neural net models can score new customers to determine the likelihood of response to product or service offerings which will be addressed in further detail in Chapter 6. It can also be used in such applications as fraud detection and default analysis.

Up to now, this book has laid the foundation of data mining principals, where they came from, the technology of today, the steps to conducting a credible mining analysis and some examples of when to apply specific methodologies. The second part of this work will focus more on the applied side of mining by offering a more detailed explanation of how mining is used in some popular business applications. It will end by providing an overall methodology on how to best implement mining and business intelligence technology in an enterprise environment and offer some clues as to what is in the pipeline for the future.

REFERENCES

Hoptroff, Richard (1992). The Principals and Practice of Time Series Forecasting and Business Modeling Using Neural Nets, *Neural Computing and Applications*, Springer-Verlag, 1(1).

Makridakis, S., Wheelright, S. C. & McGee, V.E. (1983). *Forecasting: methods and applications* 2nd edition, John Wiley & Sons, New York.

Shim, J.K, Siegel, J & Liew C.J. (1994). *Strategic Business Forecasting,* Probus Publishing, Chicago.

Part II:

Prevalent Applications
in the
World of Commerce

Chapter V

A Closer Look at Marketing/ Advertising, Promotions and Pricing Policies Using Econometric Based Modeling

Two core business strategies throughout the realm of commerce, which take their root from traditional economic theory, involve the incorporation of marketing, advertising and pricing policies for corresponding products and services. The determination of optimal strategies for each of these concepts is crucial since they account for the success or failure for a particular product or products and potentially the well being of the organization. As you well know, even the best product or service that has been mismarketed or inappropriately priced has little chance to achieve success in the market place. This is illustrated by the recent success of Ford Motor Company and their implementation of smart pricing.

> While most companies have gotten savvy about cutting costs, few have figured out how much money they are giving up by using lunkheaded pricing strategies. Lacking detailed information about market demand and their own supply capabilities, companies routinely overprice some products and underprice others. The new strategy of smart pricing draws on microeconomics, buyer psychology, and the computing power to sift through lots of data on spending patterns.[1]

The following section illustrates how regression and neural network methodologies can be used to identify optimal advertising and pricing strategies. This process can also be termed as "econometric modeling" (briefly addressed in Chapter 2) because of the more direct connection between economic theory, business strategy and statistical/quantitative analytics which verify cause and effect relationships between variables. The following chapter therefore incorporates a high-level analysis to more adequately address these crucial aspects of business strategy.

REGRESSION/NEURAL NETWORKS FOR MARKETING ANALYSIS

Basics to Mining Methodologies

Regression is the practice of attempting to fit a close fitting line or curve to data. Take, for example, the monthly sales of a hypothetical product. Suppose a scatter chart were plotted (Figure 5.1) with sales on the y axis and price on the x axis, and each monthly record being plotted as a dot:

Figure 5.1.

The eye can see a relationship here. Linear regression is a simple mathematical algorithm for expressing that pattern as a straight line through the data:

Figure 5.2.

The details of the process are discussed in Makridakis (1983) and Spurr (1973). Provided the "Steps for Success" given earlier in this book are followed, the method can generally be assumed to fit the best line to the data. The method is directional: it assumes that the quantity on the x-axis (known as the driver variable or independent variable) is driving the quantity on the y-axis (the performance measure, target or dependent variable).

By putting a driving factor on the x-axis (such as price) and a performance measure on the y-axis (such as sales), the line can be exploited in two ways:

- Examination of the cross-section makes it possible to measure how one factor influences another, e.g., how price drives sales. (It cannot explain the direction of the causal link, e.g., whether price drives sales or vice versa. Only common sense can do that.)
- It can be used for prediction, e.g., to estimate what sales would be expected at a particular price (Figure 5.3). (Care should be taken not to extrapolate far outside the range of the data.) The following chart demonstrates the principle:

Figure 5.3.

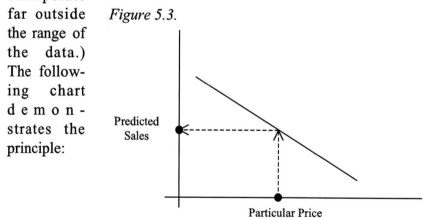

There are three major advances to basic linear regression. The first is to allow several driving factors. For example, the combined effect of pricing and advertising on sales can be determined. This is called multiple regression and it turns the line into a multidimensional surface (Figure 5.4):

Figure 5.4.

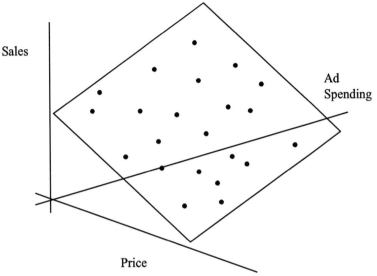

In this case, given a particular price level and advertising spending, the expected sales can be predicted. Clearly, as the number of driving factors increases, the surface gets harder to visualize. As a consequence, it is usual to just chart one driving factor at a time, and the others are assumed to be held at a constant value. These are called cross-sections. If multiple driving factors are introduced, the user has to take care that they are not linearly dependent. (This is discussed in the "Steps of Success" section of this book.)

The second advance is to allow categorical variables (e.g., North, South) to be driving factors (Figure 5.5). The trick is to treat each category as a separate driving factor. Each driving factor is zero, unless its category has been selected, in which case it takes the value one. Each category must occur at least twice in order to be usable. Any singletons should be grouped together into an "Other" category. Since the driving factors are very limited in the values they can take, the data can be compressed into a single bar chart:

Figure 5.5.

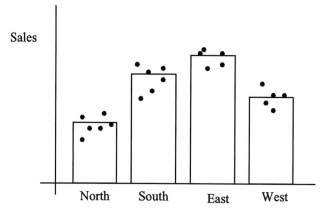

The final advance in regression is to fit curved lines rather than straight ones (Figure 5.6), a task which is also well suited for neural networks:

Figure 5.6.

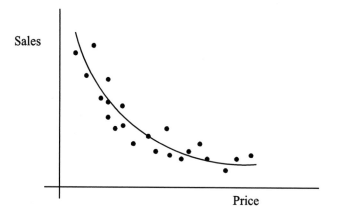

Fitting curves is more complex than it initially appears. It is not sufficient to aim to get a very good fit to the data. A very squiggly line could be made to go exactly through all the points, but it would not be much good for prediction: it would have learned the data by rote rather than capturing the underlying pattern. This is why it is emphasized in this book that tweaking an algorithm in order to obtain a better fit to the data is likely to deteriorate the result.

Few curve-fitting algorithms are able to effectively trade-off between goodness of fit and curve simplicity. Neural network curve fitting algorithms (see, for example, Wasserman, 1989, Hoptroff, 1995) are among the most effective, particularly if they actively manage the trade-off using an out-of-sample test set (Hoptroff, 1992).

MEASURING THE IMMEDIATE IMPACT OF ADVERTISING

Most advertising is designed either to have a specific, immediate effect, or to have a longer term, brand building effect. Different approaches are necessary in each case in order to quantify the effectiveness of advertising.

A good example of immediate-impact advertising is direct response advertising, (i.e. ad with reply forms.) In this case, the primary business channel is the advertisement itself. Similarly, the effect is likely to be immediate if the advertisement announces a short-lived promotion or price reduction. Measurement of the effect of such campaigns is straightforward because the impact is immediate.

In order to quantify the impact of advertising in a business, it will be necessary to collect data on the factors that affect sales, including advertising, and to fit a curve in order to understand how they drive the performance measure. The performance measure could be brand awareness data obtained through market research (Hoptroff, 1997). However, a more direct approach is to use sales units. Examining the cross-section of advertising against sales units will quantify the immediate impact that advertising has had on the business. This will allow its bottom line effectiveness to be calculated.

The process of measuring the instantaneous effectiveness of advertising on sales will be demonstrated using sales data for a well-known consumer goods product. Monthly sales data for the product are available. (The data are millions of units):

Figure 5.7.

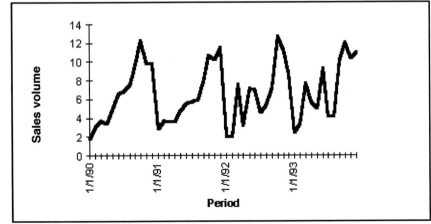

Several driving factors are also available – Advertising Spending:
Figure 5.8.

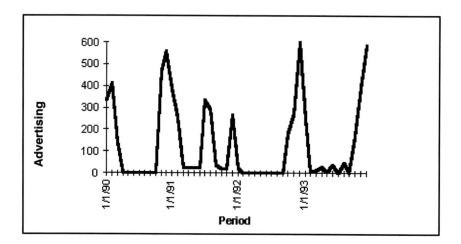

Promotional Spending:

Figure 5.9.

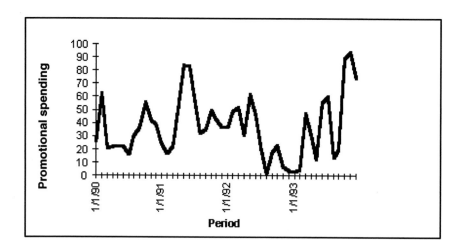

Price:

Figure 5.10.

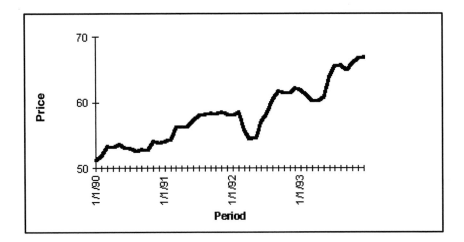

Average Competitor Price:

Figure 5.11.

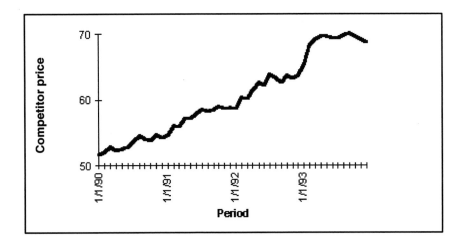

These factors were used as driving factors to fit a curve to the sales data using an off-the-self neural network curve-fitting program. The sales data is clearly seasonal, (Figure 5.12), so the name of the month was also included as a category variable. Its cross-section indicates the inherent seasonality of sales, with all other factors held constant:

Figure 5.12.

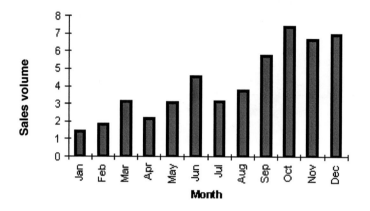

The seasonal factor was included so that seasonal variations were accounted for. It might have further use in a forecasting role (as was illustrated in Chapter 4), but it has no further use here. The other cross sections are more useful. First, examine the advertising cross-section in Figure 5.13:

Figure 5.13.

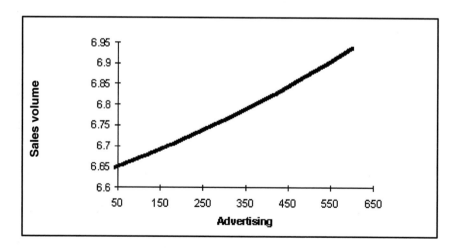

The impact is clear and positive, but is it enough? Increasing advertising spending from 50 to 650 units has boosted sales from 6.65 million to 6.95 million or a 5% increase. In order to measure the benefit, it is necessary to incorporate knowledge about the cost C dollars per unit of the advertising and the dollar margin per unit M obtained on the increased sales. The dollar return R on advertising is then:

$$R = \frac{M \times (6950000 - 6650000)}{C \times (650 - 50)} \quad \text{dollars return per dollar spent}$$

For example, if M, the margin per unit sold, was 25¢ and C, the cost per unit of advertising was $100, the dollar return would be $1.25, or a 25% return on investment.

MEASURING THE IMPACT
OF PRICE AND PROMOTIONS

The impact of promotions can be examined in the same way. The cross-section obtained for promotions in this example is:

Figure 5.14.

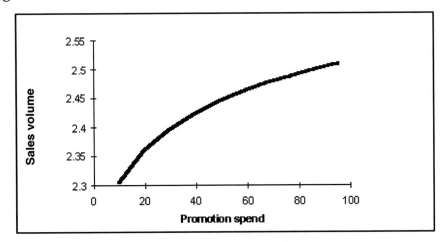

In the figure above, the cross-section is more curved. It is more beneficial to increase the promotional spending from 10 to 30 than from 60 to 80. As in the previous example, the dollar return on promotions can be calculated. However, since the line is curved, the dollar return will vary with promotional spending. Using a similar methodology as before, and assuming a cost of promotions of $500 dollars per unit, the following return curve is obtained:

Figure 5.15.

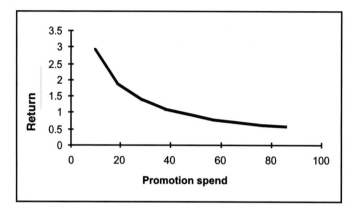

At a promotional spending of around 50 units, the dollar return falls below $1 per dollar, i.e., less than the amount invested. This marks the limit to positive returns to promotions in this case.

In a similar manner, the impact of price can be assessed. The cross-section obtained for price in this example is a classic price elasticity curve:

Figure 5.16.

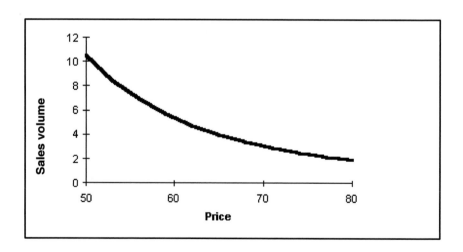

Increasing the price has a significant impact on sales. The process of using this type of curve to determine the optimum price is discussed in the next chapter.

MEASURING THE LONGER TERM
IMPACT OF ADVERTISING

Longer term advertising is primarily intended to win people over to a particular product or brand. The product is usually purchased through some other business channel. It is less likely that such an advertisement will increase overall market demand; its effect is more likely to win brand share over the long term. (For example, advertising an automobile is not likely to make someone rush out and buy one, but one could reasonably hope that the next time they made an automobile purchase, they would buy that brand.)

Measuring the effect of such campaigns is trickier than immediate-impact campaigns, but it is possible. The key to it is to look for patterns in sales growth rather than sales. (This is discussed more rigorously in Hoptroff, 1997).

To understand sales growth, the performance measure will be the difference in sales from one month to the next. The driving factors should include advertising and other factors thought to impact sales. They should also include sales in order to allow the system to steady itself. The impact of sales on sales growth will turn out to be negative, so that if sales are low there will be pressure on them to grow; while if they are too high, they will tend to decline. All other things staying constant, sales will level off at some equilibrium point. This equilibrium point will be determined by the other factors such as advertising. Readers familiar with calculus will recognize this as an evolutionary differential approach.

An example will help to clarify the approach. The data are annual sales for a confectionery manufacturer:

Figure 5.17.

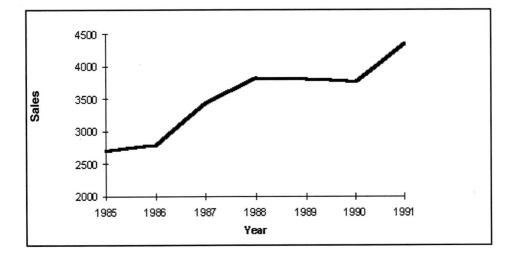

Data also available are the advertising spending:

Figure 5.18.

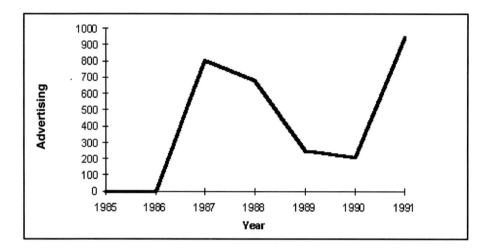

And the distribution penetration (the percentage of potential outlets who actually stock the item):

Figure 5.19.

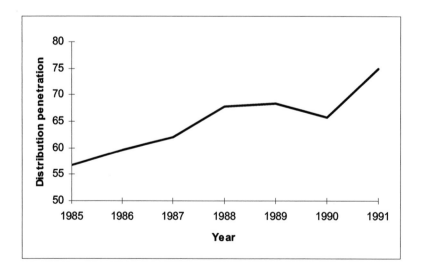

A regression model was built using sales growth as the performance measure and sales, advertising and distribution as the driving factors. Consider first the relationship between sales and sales growth:

Figure 5.20.

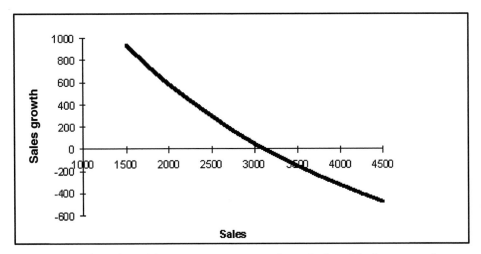

Remember that this curve represents the relationship between the two variables while holding distribution and advertising at constant values (70 and 500 respectively). Whatever the initial value of sales, there will be a drift over time towards a level of 3100, where the line crosses the x-axis. (If the current level of sales is higher than this, sales growth is negative and vice versa.)

Now look at the same cross-section when advertising is held at a constant level of zero:

Figure 5.21.

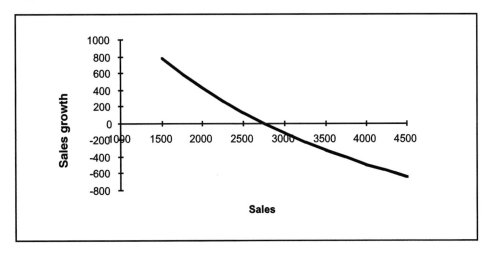

Now the equilibrium level is 2750. Therefore if advertising is increased from 0 to 500, we would expect sales to grow – over the longer term – to 3,100. This is the essence of the longer term regression approach.

In order to measure the longer term payoff of advertising, the regression model is used to run simulations to predict sales with and without spending money on advertising. In this example, two simulations were run. The first predicted the level of sales with no advertising (but the actual level of distribution during the period.) The second included the advertising spending of 1992 and then cut future spending to zero:

Figure 5.22.

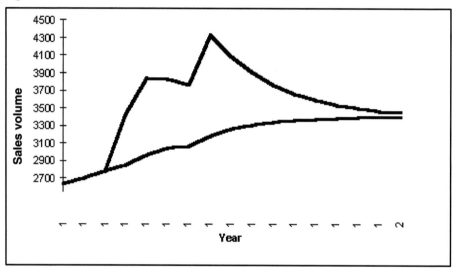

In this chart above, the upper line represents the sales with advertising, the lower one without. Note that sales decays only slowly to an equilibrium level after advertising is cut in 1992. Such is the longer-term impact of the advertising. The return on advertising up to 1992 is given by the area between the two lines.

Other Techniques to Measure Longer Term Impacts of Advertising on Target Measures

Other applications, which incorporate the measurement (cost) of advertising, involve the application of lags (how does advertising this month affect revenue next month). This can be done by merely incorporating lagged coefficients of the advertising variable on the target measure of revenue, units or market share. Another method to address the issue of impacts of past advertising expenditure entails the calculation of a "Smoothed Measure" which can be estimated by applying a moving average of advertising expenditure over a number of periods (e.g., this month's, last month's and 2 months previous expenditure on advertising). This result is then incorporated as the independent variable for the corresponding target variable. Regardless of the measure, however, the methodology remains consistent with that mentioned in this section.

Examples for lags and smoothed advertising measures:

Year	Month	Ad Spending	Revenue
1999	Jan	210	780,000
1999	Feb	225	810,000
1999	Mar	200	815,000
1999	Apr	230	910,000
1999	May	235	928,000

Lagged driving variables for regression or neural network models could incorporate the three months of Jan, Feb and March 1999 (Ad Spending) as independent variables on March 1999 revenue (target variable) going forward for the model building process.

Smoothed advertising driving variables could incorporate a moving average beginning with the three month average of (Jan., Feb., March) for Ad Spending on March revenue as a target.

A CLOSER LOOK AT PRICING STRATEGIES

In the last section we made reference to the affects of pricing in the overall, multivariate model of marketing and advertising. The following section will address the issue of pricing policies in its own space by focusing on optimal product pricing determination with the use of regression or neural networks once again. This topic illustrates the clear connection between micro economic theory (marginal cost) and business strategy with the aid of analytical technology.

Price Optimization Using Cross-Sections: Data Mining For Pricing

The pricing decision is a delightful application of data mining. Pricing decisions are often decided unscientifically and can often deviate far from the optimum. The analysis is generally quick and easy. The implementation of the result – an adjustment in price – is painless and can boost profits immediately and significantly. However, this assumes that an accurate analysis using appropriate technology has been conducted.

The types of results demonstrated in this chapter can be obtained using any regression tool which incorporates a spreadsheet.

Price Elasticity

In the previous section, a regression model was built that identified, among other things, the impact of price on the sales of a product:

Figure 5.23.

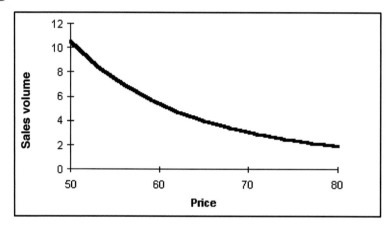

This cross section shows that as the price increases, sales steadily decrease. It is known as a price elasticity curve. The steeper a curve is, the more sensitive customers are to price. In this case the curve is quite smooth, but this is by no means certain (Hoptroff, 1998).

The price elasticity curve obtained using regression or neural networks may be used to set prices. The price should be a tactical choice within the range of two limits:

- The optimum or profit-maximizing price, being the price at which the most profit is made.
- The break-even price, being the lowest price for which the product line does not make a loss.

In a stable market, the profit-maximizing price should be charged. A product manager can increase market share by lowering the price, although this will be at the expense of short-term profits.

Common business strategy asserts that price should not be lowered below the break-even price. To do so is considered to be a practice called predatory pricing. This is not to say that in today's information economy, given the presence of (.com) start-ups and the existence of the potential for peripheral revenue streams, that below break even activity is not out of the question.

Finding The Optimum And Break-Even Prices

Both price levels may be determined using the price elasticity curve. It is also necessary to determine how costs increase as sales increase. In some cases this can be estimated in terms of fixed and variable costs by examination of the general ledger and estimating which costs are fixed and which are proportional to the level of sales:

Figure 5.24.

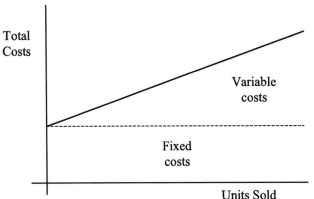

It is also possible to determine the relationship by building a regression or neural net model of how the costs vary according to the number of units sold. In this case, total costs would be the performance measure and sales units would be the only driving factor. (Since costs vary somewhat sluggishly, it would be sensible to look over the longer term—i.e., each record might be a quarter, rather than a week or a month.) The relationship between costs and unit sales is then given by the cross-section:

Figure 5.25.

(In this case, no greater detail than a straight-line relationship could be found. This is not always necessarily the case (Hoptroff, 1998).) Next, it is necessary to know how costs vary with price. This is achieved by combining this cross-section with the one obtained previously, which related units sold to price, in order to relate costs and price directly:

Figure 5.26.

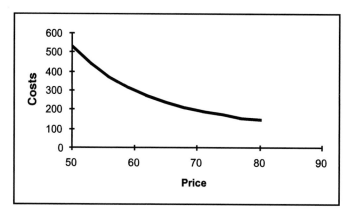

Similarly, the relationship between sales revenues and price is required. Since the sales revenues are simply the sale units multiplied by the selling price, this curve is easily obtained:

Figure 5.27.

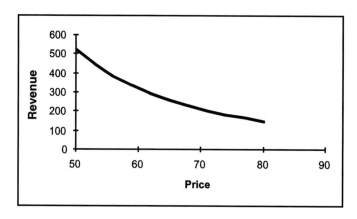

Finally, subtracting the costs curve from the revenue curve yields the desired profit-price relationship:

Figure 5.28.

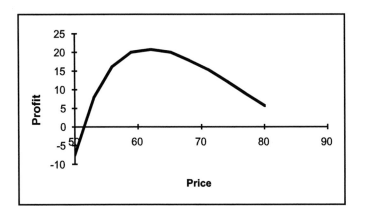

The profit-maximizing price is given by the peak in the curve: around 62¢. The break-even price is where the line crosses the x-axis: around 52¢. In order to maximize profit, a price of between 59¢ and 65¢ should be charged. (The profit curve is quite flat at the peak, so a few cents either way does not make much difference.) In order to gain market share, the price could be lowered as far as 52¢, but this would have an increasingly dramatic impact on profits. Below 52¢, the product operates at a loss and the seller is engaging in predatory pricing.

It is often asked why a multi-stage process is necessary. Why not, for example, build a direct regression or neural net model of profit against price? The reason is that two separate relationships are at play: how much it costs to produce different quantities of a product, and how many customers will buy the product at a given price level. These individual relationships are strong and easily determined using a data mining system.

When the two are combined, they largely cancel each other out, leaving behind a more delicate, complex (i.e., strongly curved) relationship. It will be much harder for a data mining system to extract this pattern from data that is in any way noisy or erratic.

The above analysis was based on one cross-section. Therefore it is appropriate only for the values of competitor price, advertising expenditure, etc., for which the cross-section was created. If any of these values change, the cross-sections will change. The regression tool (or a spreadsheet) can be used to track the optimum price as conditions change. Keep in mind the importance of the preceding section since it can be applied to such strategies as smart pricing mentioned at the beginning of the chapter.

A BRIEF MENTION OF OTHER REGRESSION AND NEURAL NETWORK APPLICATIONS

The preceding sections concentrated mainly on the application of regression and neural network approaches to the critical issues of marketing, advertising and price analysis along with forecasting applications. These mining methodologies can be utilized in a host of business related scenarios that require predictive modeling.

Market Research Analysis

Questionnaires, field interviews, conjoint analysis and focus group results can be analyzed to understand the relationship between different questions.

Each respondent constitutes a record in the analysis. The research should be designed so that some of the questions make sense as performance measures. For example, "How often you dine out each week?" The remaining questions then ask about factors which might be drivers, such as, "How many hours do you work a week?"

The regression or neural network model will show the driving factors in more detail than most other analyses, which tend to look at one driving factor at a time. The fact that these approaches look at all the driving factors together, however, yields a greater advantage: smaller sample sizes are needed for a given level of detail. This means the cost of research can be reduced.

To understand the potential for reducing sample sizes in market research, try putting the results of an existing survey through a regression system. (Use one with out-of-sample testing since these work well with smaller quantities of data.) First verify that the regression model agrees with the conclusions of your market research. Then discard half the records, chosen at random, and rebuild the model. It will probably not be noticeably different, yet would have cost half as much to conduct.

Personnel Performance And Retention (HR)

The performance of different members of a team can be measured and attributed to different causal factors such as training, compensation, experience, etc. This is used to identify what people can do to improve their performance.

Each record in the data is a person in a particular job role (at least 20 or 30 people will be needed). The performance measure will vary between job roles; a salesperson's performance is readily given by the sales they generate. Other employees may have more qualitative measures such as ratings in their personnel files. In order to understand the factors which drive employee retention, the performance measure will be months with the company.

The driving factors should include factors under the employer's control such as training, perks, working hours, compensation and recognition. If possible, these factors should be expressed in terms of their dollar cost so that their cross-sections may be directly compared to determine; for example, whether bonus or a free holiday has a better impact on employee retention. Personnel applications are not limited to the above scenarios but can include such topics as employee attrition or retirement trends.

Personnel Selection

Just as regression or neural networks may be used to improve the performance of existing employees, it can be used to develop hiring criteria for future employees. The analysis is still performed on the existing employees. The main difference is that the driving factors should be data that are available at the time of hiring – ideally, on the resumé. Factors could include academic qualifications, experience, time out of work, average job tenure, etc. Personal factors such as age and sex may also be effective but their use may be restricted by legal and ethical limitations.

The resulting regression model will provide cross-sections that will indicate how important the driving factors should be to a hiring decision. The potential of new applicants may then be predicted by feeding their details into the corresponding model.

This approach has also been used in schools and universities to understand what drives academic excellence and to aid the admissions selection process.

Retail Outlet Location Analysis

Just as regression or neural networks are used to determine which candidate employees are most likely to perform well, it can be used to predict the performance of potential locations for new retail outlets.

Each record in the database will be an existing retail outlet. A suitable performance measure might be revenue or profit for that location, but since the locations are likely to vary in size, it might be smarter to work with revenue or profit per square foot.

Driving factors might include size, number of people passing the store-front each day, number of floors, parking availability, etc. (They must be factors that are available for candidate locations, too.) The model will then show the relative importance of these factors. The potential of new sites can be predicted by feeding details into the corresponding model.

Business Unit Analysis

If a business can be broken up into distinct units such as retail outlets or sales offices, their performance can be analyzed to identify how to improve performance. This analysis is particularly appealing because much of the data is available in the general ledger in terms of income and expense items.

Each record will be a business unit. The performance measure will probably be revenue, production or profit for a profit center and costs for a cost center. If the business units vary in size, the performance measure should be normalized, e.g., revenue per person (i.e., productivity).

The driving factors will vary according to business, but might include cultural differences between business units, working hours, production methods, infrastructure, training etc. The cross-sections of the resulting model will help identify the relative benefits of various business practices. For example, what impact does information technology have on production?

There is no reason why the business units need to come from the same company. If the data are available, it is possible to analyze competing companies in this way in order to understand competitive advantage in fragmented markets.

Closing Thoughts

As you can see, the applicability of high-end, predictive and cause-effect measuring methodologies of regression and neural networks is far reaching. It is the purpose of this book to enlighten the business community on how to apply these types of technologies to reduce uncertainty in the marketplace. More specifically, this past chapter has provided an overview on how economic theory, business strategy and analytical technology are applied together to achieve optimal strategies to survive in the market place. Survivability in this case refers to achieving an increased level of efficiency in the firms' day-to-day operations.

The next chapter will step ahead and address driving applications more unique to the evolving information economy or e-business applications. It provides a nice link from the more traditional "brick-and-mortar" style firm to the quickly growing "click-and-mortar" organizations (click and mortar refers to the increased utilization of the Internet by companies in all industries) and incorporates such mining methodologies as profiling and market basket analysis to help transform data into information that augments business intelligence.

ENDNOTES

[1] Coy Peter, "The Power of Smart Pricing," *BusinessWeek Magazine*, McGraw-Hill, April, 2000.

REFERENCES

Berry, M.J.A. and Linoff, G. (1997). *Data Mining Techniques for Marketing, Sales and Customer Support,* Wiley Computer Publishing, New York.

Hoptroff, Richard (1996). The Principles and Practice of Time Series Forecasting and Business Modeling Using Neural Nets, *Neural Computing and Applications,* Springer-Verlag, 1(1).

Hoptroff, Richard (1995). Neural Network Case Studies in Marketing Analysis, *Journal of Targeting, Measurement and Analysis for Marketing*, Henry Stewart, London, 3(3).

Hoptroff, Richard, Williams, M. & Barak, N. (1997). Contemporary Approaches to Quantifying Advertising Effectiveness, *Journal of Targeting Measurement and Analysis for Marketing,* Henry Stewart, London, 5(4).

Hoptroff, Richard, Nairn, D.W. & Shepherd A.M. (1998). Practical Approaches to Pricing Analysis, *Journal of Targeting, Measurement and Analysis for Marketing*, Henry Stewart, London, 6(3).

Wasserman, P.D. (1983). Neural Computing—Theory and Practice, Van Norstrand Reinhold, New York, NY.

Chapter VI

Turning Your Brick and Mortar Into a "Click and Mortar"

by Engage Inc.

"As Web ventures begin to view personalization as ongoing processes rather than discrete technologies, investments should be made for building a flexible data management infrastructure that can accommodate a variety of consumer data and analytical techniques."

—Jupiter Communications, June, 2000 Report

THE ESTABLISHMENT GOES WIRED

I recently read an article about words and terms that evolved exclusively from the American culture. This piece traced the history of American-born verbiage throughout the 1900s and into the year 2000. Not surprisingly, many of the words that appeared in later years were some of the most pervasive buzzwords and terms of our Web-wild culture: e-business, e-commerce, click-and-mortar, among others. It's daunting, really; no wonder some retailers are confounded by what faces them as they ponder the move from offline to online.

You've spent millions of dollars implementing a customer relationship management system to better understand your customers: their wants, their desires, their buying habits. You've used it to great success to build excellent offline customer relations. You're now looking for the next big opportunity, the jump into something beyond what you're currently doing.

The truth is that those that *do* make the jump can be exposed to a tremendous amount of opportunity and increased revenue. Using the data that your customer relationship management (CRM) solution has collected about offline customers and "multichanneling" it, as it's called, can lead to big profits. Traditional marketers' eyes light up when they see forecasts predicting that $199 billion will have been spent by consumers online by 2005 ("Online Influencing Offline: The Multichannel Mandate," Jupiter Communications, June, 2000). The challenge presented to marketers is how to successfully make the jump to promoting their goods in cyberspace.

The thing to remember is that a lot of the same rules apply—but on the Web, you have a lot more options. Be aware that Web and offline marketing share some basic truisms. The ultimate goal is to identify your appropriate audiences and market to them accordingly. Get to know your audiences, present them information that is customized to their needs and interests, and deliver it to them in a non-intrusive manner. The Web makes it exceedingly easy to do this, especially with solutions like online profiling, which this chapter will cover in detail.

Build a brand that people can identify and associate with good things. This can be easier for traditional marketers than for pure Web plays; if you've already developed your brand offline, and it's got good name recognition, that already gives you a head-start. People expect you to bring your well-respected, high-quality service to the Web, and associate good things with your company.

There are some concerns that you must be aware of, however. Paramount to these is the issue of consumer privacy on the Web, of which there have been many recent discussions. Pay attention to these discussions. Respect the consumer's concern for anonymity. More on this later, but take heed—make this a priority by considering it a part of your customer relationship program.

These are some of the opportunities and challenges that need to be considered before turning your "brick-and-mortar" into a "click-and-mortar." This chapter will attempt to illustrate these issues in greater detail, as well as present some of the solutions that can help you meet the challenges that you face as you begin to market on the Web. It will address how to use online profiling to gain a better understanding of your Web prospects and customers, and show how a combination of profiling, CRM and analytical data can help you gain a complete view and understanding of these customers.

But that's only the beginning. Once you've identified the prospects, you need to market to them. The ability to target and modify online marketing programs on the fly, to achieve better return on investments and to convert prospects into long, loyal customers, is unique to the Web.

Finally, as mentioned earlier, privacy is an important issue, one that must not be ignored. It is possibly the greatest threat to businesses who do not understand the controversies that surround consumer online privacy. This is why companies must set standards that address this issue.

The Internet has seemingly made the world a bigger place for both consumers and marketers alike. There are huge opportunities, but if one is not careful, these opportunities can turn to dust, and a company's dreams of creating an online empire can prove to be fruitless. With knowledge, vision and the right tools, good customer relationships—and yes, profitability—can be found on the Web.

ONLINE PROFILING IS THE KEY

The basis for any marketing program is getting to know your customers as much as possible. In the offline world, customer data is collected through a number of ways, including past purchasing history, demographic research, responses derived from direct mail programs, promotions and other tactics. Customer relations—a give-and-take between customer and company—are developed with these good, proven methods, all of which are also used in the online world. But technology has made it easier than ever to identify not only audiences and demographic groups on the Web, but the interests and preferences of specific individuals. At the heart of this technology is online audience profiling. It brings the targetability of marketing programs to a completely new level, and, when used in conjunction with offline customer information that has been filtered through a data mining process, can serve as the foundation for developing a successful online CRM and marketing program.

But what is online profiling? Think of it as an art—the art of being able to become intimately familiar with a person's needs or interests. A profile is, to put it simply, a collection of information about a single online consumer. One way to build a profile is to monitor the Web pages that a user views on particular subjects, products or services and then translate that data into interests. These interests naturally change over time. If the right technology is used, the profiles will reflect changing interests and become a powerful marketing tool.

Profiles can be either personally identifiable or anonymous. Personally identifiable profiles contain information such as names, addresses or e-mail addresses, and should only be used if the user has granted consent to do so. Anonymous profiles, however, do not contain personally identifiable information. The uniqueness of the Internet makes it unnecessary to know personally identifiable information in order to effectively market to an individual. That, as well as the current concerns about online privacy, means that anonymous profiles should be embraced.

Profiles, unlike static customer data, can grow and change in step with the evolving interests of the Web user. These profiles are dynamic; they contain information which changes as a user's browsing habits change, reflecting fluctuating interest levels in particular products or services. They can be determined by three key items: the recency that a person has viewed information about a product or service online; the frequency with which they have done so; and how long they spent viewing the information. For instance, if a person is in the market for a sports utility vehicle, they may go online to get information on the different options that are out there. At this time, their online profile will register a high interest in cars and, even more granularly, SUVs. But once that person buys the SUV, chances are they won't be looking for them online as much; hence, their profile will reflect that their interest in SUVs has waned. For a marketer, this obviously becomes very valuable information—the SUV marketer can optimize their marketing campaign so that they're hitting the consumer at the appropriate time, and when that consumer's interest wanes, they can focus their efforts on hitting a different target that continues to show a strong interest in their product.

"Interest scores" provide insight into the products and services that an individual is seeking information on. These scores are at the heart of profiling. In the SUV example, if a numerical interest score scale from .01 to 1.0 is used, with 1.0 being the number that signifies the highest interest, that number will decrease after the consumer purchases the car.

Underlying the profiles can be some very complicated proprietary software. How much do you need to know how it works? You don't have to understand differential equations to take a car around a curve, but you better turn the wheel to reflect the concept or you will end up over a cliff. Similarly, although interest scores are a simple concept, they are actually the result of complex mathematical functions that allow them to change over time; for example, if the consumer hasn't expressed interest in a particular category recently, they should not be marketed products and services from that category.

What companies venturing online need to realize is that people aren't just interested in one or two things. After all, just because a person is surfing a golf site doesn't mean they're not interested in cooking, too.

This is why the interest information within a profile can be arranged into categories. These categories can have many different levels that serve to provide ever-greater detail about a person's interests, allowing marketers to get very targeted and granular in their campaigns. For example, one category might be an overarching—and fairly extensive—Auto category. But that can be broken into subcategories, where a user who shows an interest in "Autos" may have an interest in, more specifically, "Sports Utility Vehicles," and, even more granularly, Chevy Tahoes. The profiling hierarchy allows marketers to get a very clear view of the specific interests and to target them with whatever precision they need.

Make no mistake, profiling provides many benefits. These benefits increase when marketers who are moving online can take their offline data and, with a user's permission, overlay it with the interest and behavioral information contained in a profile. This is stretching the data that you have mined so that it becomes valuable not only in your offline campaigns, but also in your online marketing programs. Together, the profile and permission-based offline data can provide a complete, 360 degree view of your online customers.

THE 360° CUSTOMER VIEW

"A single view of each customer is cited as a critical or very important business need, but only 2% of firms have it today...Companies need a new approach—eRelationship management—to leverage the Web's unique strengths for capturing and publishing a single view of customers."

— *Forrester Research, June, 1999 Report*

How much do you want to bet that companies within that 2% are getting better returns than those that aren't? Now the question arises, don't you want to be in that 2%—both offline *and* online?

Transferring your offline campaigns to online is not as easy as it may appear. One of the chief reasons for this is that people's habits change when they get online. For instance, my wife can go grocery shopping quicker than anyone, but get her on Peapod.com and she likes to take her time and browse. This opens up more possibilities for the marketer, but it also makes it challenging—how do you market to someone whose interests can show so many variables? Which is why a highly targeted program becomes even more critical online.

The good news is that if you have a data mining program in place, you've already won half the battle. You've already built the foundation for a successful online marketing program.

Think of your data mining solution as your million dollar building blocks that have developed your foothold for moving online. Specifically, think of them as *three* building blocks, each serving a different analytical function as it relates to the customer relationship: transaction history (what customers bought), customer history (how they've interacted with your company) and customer call center (what they related to). Each collects its own crucial pieces of information about your customers, all of which come together to give you a pretty detailed offline view. The information in these can be combined with, but may not be limited to, customer names, geographical locations, and purchasing preferences, all collected with the customers' permission.

Contained in the data warehouse, this information can be used in the entire CRM operation. The data can be analyzed to form the basis of an offline marketing program. This analysis helps determine which customers get which promotional offers, direct mail pieces, and where advertisements can be targeted. Once these programs are implemented, the CRM operation monitors their success (or lack thereof) and reports it back to the company. This allows the programs to be optimized as necessary. This action falls under the definition of campaign management.

It's all meant to create a single customer view—offline. That view is then used to target campaigns via the traditional mediums, including print, TV, radio, catalogs, and others.

When a company becomes a click-and-mortar, these tactics still play a big role. But other options begin opening themselves up to you. If 150 million people come online over the next couple of years, that's a potential 150 million customers, depending on the services you're pitching. And as I've stated before, the best way to pitch your customer is to know them as well as possible. In order to get to these people, you need solutions that harness the power of the Web to expand your marketing opportunities. This means incorporating online behavior and interest, user profiles and combining this information with the data that you have already collected about your customers throughout your data mining process. By doing this, you can gain a complete, 360 degree view of your customers, whether they are online or offline, and tailor your messaging, promotions and merchandising in very specific ways.

Let's use an example of how this may work. You're a sports clothing manufacturer whose offline customer-centric view shows that Customer A lives in Salt Lake City, Utah, and has a history of purchasing ski equipment: ski gloves, jacket, etc. But you sell other types of clothing, not just ski apparel. Still, this is all you know about Customer A.

When you move online, you begin to use profiles to gain a better understanding of each of your customers. One profile shows a user that has visited sites pertaining to ski areas around Utah using a local online guide. This person has also shown a high interest in restaurants in the Salt Lake City area—indicating a strong chance that they may actually live in Salt Lake City—as well as strong interest in ski equipment. This could very well be Customer A, or, if it isn't, somebody who shares similar interests.

But wait a second. This same user also shows a relatively strong interest in other types of athletic equipment—golf clubs, for instance. Big Berthas, to be precise. And they've just recently researched them on the Web. You just happen to carry Big Berthas. And now you know that Customer A might be an appropriate target for marketing your golf wares.

Would you have known this without online profiling? Probably not, at least not until the person made a purchase from your golf shop. Maybe that person isn't even aware of your golf offerings. With the complete, 360 degree customer view, they can be. So now, with a better knowledge of the interests of Customer A, you can enhance your marketing programs to them both online *and* offline—one hand washing the other.

Of course, I'm not just referring to ads here. All types of marketing are to be considered, including promotions. Offline promotions targeted using customer data can be translated to the Web through a combination of offline and online information. Direct e-mail special offers can bet tailored to appeal to the customer on-the-fly, as their interests change. All of this should and can be done while maintaining a consistent brand both in your traditional marketing and on the Web. Plus, these programs can become even more effective when the offline data—for example, names and addresses—is overlayed with anonymous profiles. However, and this will be discussed in greater detail further on, it is worth pointing out that this should only be done with the express consent of the user.

MODIFY & CONVERT

The targeting is just one aspect of the online marketing program, however. Measurability is just as crucial online as it is offline. The good news is that online it is actually easier and quicker to measure the true effectiveness of ad campaigns because this measurement can be done in real-time. What used to take months to test and longer to implement can now happen in a matter of days. For instance, if you're experiencing what we call high click-through rates on your banner ad campaigns—with high click-through being the number of people clicking on your ads and jumping to your Web site—

those responses can be monitored as they happen. But, if you're finding that no one, or a relatively small number of people are clicking on your ads, you can change that campaign relatively quickly, whether to retarget it to a different audience or begin placing the ads in different locations from where they currently are. The point, once again, is that you have more flexibility with your online programs than with your offline, which can lead to a greater opportunity for success.

The goal is to create an online campaign that grabs the attention of the user and won't let them go, so that they're driven to some sort of action. In most cases, that ideal call to action would be a purchase, or at least a response to a promotion that may ultimately result in a purchase. The beauty of online marketing is that you can determine what's working and what isn't faster than you can with your offline promotions. So if you're not receiving click-through with an audience that you're trying to reach, or if you're not converting visitors to your site into customers, ad campaign measurement and analytical solutions can help you modify your programs appropriately, to increase your chances of success.

Reporting and analysis software is used to measure a variety of things, from the number of times a user may have clicked on an ad to the number of impressions the ad has registered (the number of times an ad appeared on a site). It can tell you how many people like Offer X but not Offer Y, or that Customer A likes Offer X, but Customer B likes Offer Y. New tools can even measure the effectiveness of simply viewing an ad and how creative and branding can help drive customers to your site. The optimization of traditional offline marketing campaigns and promotions begs either conjecture (sales haven't increased over a period of X months, therefore there must be something wrong with my promotional material) or response (I started this direct mail campaign three months ago, and have only gotten a .2% response rate—something's got to change). Online measurement and analysis can cut a three month response time down to a couple of days, at least on the Internet. When you combine profiles with offline customer data, this type of information can also give you an early heads-up of either success or troubles that may lie ahead in both your online *and* offline programs; if you launch a full-scale marketing program both on and offline, and the online aspect isn't working, chances are it's not going to work offline, either. If you know your online results faster, it could give you a chance to modify your offline program, as well, before you spend an inordinate amount of money on something that's not going to get to the appropriate audience. Once again, the combination of data can help your online and offline efforts feed on each other, helping you make the most out of all your marketing campaigns.

A WORD ON PRIVACY

Online privacy is not to be taken lightly. This is one of the first rules you must become familiar with as you begin using your offline data in the online world.

As of this writing, the Federal Trade Commission (FTC) is seriously considering imposing legislation that will regulate how companies can market their products and services over the Web. Companies are, in turn, promoting the benefits of industry self-regulation as a means to continue to provide users with a free Web and maintain the explosive growth in e-commerce that we've been enjoying for the past couple of years.

At the crux of this debate is the issue of whether or not names, addresses, and other personally identifiable information should be combined with anonymous user information—such as that contained within the aforementioned anonymous profiles—without a user's consent. It should not. Plain and simple.

This is why privacy is a big issue for all Web companies, but should be of particular concern to businesses that are considering using customer data culled through offline methods in conjunction with online marketing. While it's true that the combination of anonymous profiling information collected on the Web and information obtained from data mining can be a powerful one, companies need to take steps *before* making this combination a reality. In fact, the FTC has drawn up several Fair Information Practices that it is recommended that companies follow very closely:

- Notice—always provide consumers with notice of the data you are collecting and how you are using this data. Online, this includes, but is not relegated to, the posting of detailed, clearly understood and clearly visible Web site privacy statements.
- Choice—always provide consumers with the choice of opting out (that is, become exempt to the collection of) such data collection. Make it easy for them to do so. If you're planning on collecting personally identifiable data, only do so if the consumer has voluntarily opted into such a collection. The same applies for companies that plan on combining offline customer data with anonymous user profiles. Only share data with third-parties if the user has authorized it.
- Access—always provide consumers with access to their data, whenever they want to view it, so that they know their information is being handled properly and correctly.
- Security—always provide security around the data. No one wants their personally identifiable information accessed by a third-party that does not have authorization from the user to do so.

It behooves companies to abide by these guidelines. First, none of these prohibit the success of an online marketing program. In fact, they can only serve to elevate you in the eyes of the consumer. Trust is as much of a part of marketing as targeting, measurement, or anything else. Trust looms even larger on the Internet, because even though it's become a ubiquitous part of our lives, the Web is still something that the average consumer has only the most cursory understanding of.

Second, the heat is very high right now, and does not promise to cool down any time soon. The government, the press, consumer advocates, and the consumers themselves—all are taking a hard-line stance against companies that do not respect the concerns of the general public when it comes to online privacy, and rightfully so. The magnifying glass is much more focused on the world of online advertising than it is in the traditional world right now, so all companies need to be careful—but especially the ones who plan on using offline data (even if their customers have *volunteered* this data)—for online marketing purposes.

I encourage you to seek further information on industry organizations that have been designed to promote self-regulation and help companies in these efforts. Organizations like TRUSTe (www.truste.org), the Online Privacy Alliance (www.opa.org) and the Network Advertising Initiative (www.networkadvertising.org) are all worth a close look.

TO INFINITY...AND BEYOND

I am all for a first-things-first approach. Focus on developing your move onto the Web by taking a hard look at what needs to be done on, for lack of a better word, "traditional" Web sites that are delivered over desktop PCs. But when you're doing this, bear in mind that these are just the tip of the iceberg.

I snap my fingers; the Internet changes. It evolves. It has done this for the past twenty years, but now it's really picking up steam. The desktop is still viable, and probably always will be, but the Web visionaries are now looking at other devices to help them reach the end user, and more and more tech-savvy businesses are taking a hard look at new ways of helping them increase revenue online.

For example, Jupiter Communications predicts that there will be over 75 million Internet-enabled cell phones in use by 2003, up from 27 million in 2001. With cell phone screens getting larger, online marketing via cell phones is quickly becoming an attractive proposition for advertisers. Let's go back to the previous example of the sporting goods Salt Lake City customer who, through profiling, we found likes golf equipment. What if, when they powered up their Palm Pilot and logged onto the Web, they were served an ad that promotes a sale on Big Bertha clubs at one of your retail locations in the Salt Lake City area? This is not intrusive to the consumer; regardless of the fact that it's on their Palm Pilot, they're receiving information on something that is targeted directly at one of their major interests. And there's a good chance that you've got another new customer driving to your retail outlet, Palm Pilot in hand.

The interesting thing is that a Palm Pilot's Web browser can contain a cookie, which means that the user of the Palm Pilot can be profiled. However, this is entirely up to the carrier that is providing the service. As of this writing, not all providers allow cookies. However, it is my opinion that the sites that are pioneering wireless Web sites will also experience the benefits of targeted wireless advertising. Their success, spurred by advertising, will encourage others to follow suit. Once this happens, the carriers themselves will also see the value of profiling, and will begin to allow for the use of cookies through their services.

Cell phones aren't the only device. Traditional marketing methods that you've used in the past, such as television and radio commercials, print ads, direct mail pieces and catalogs, have given way to desktop, online advertising, which then gives way to cell phones…and personal digital assistants…and pagers…and enhanced televisions…and in-store kiosks…and gas pumps. All ads and promotions relevant to the consumer and targeted directly to them.

Make no mistake; this is not going to be a quick transition. It will probably take another year before most of these applications start to gain acceptance. But the movement is happening right now. Europe is a good example. Already well-known for its advancements in the wireless industry, ads over cell phones are starting to become a common practice overseas, embraced by both marketers and users alike. Also, in Japan, devices inspired by electronic games but have the functionality of cell phones and Palm Pilots are proving to be hugely popular. That acceptance will slowly take hold here in the U.S. Ads over other technologies, such as enhanced TV, will be driven by consumer adoption of those technologies and the growth of the particular markets. But once consumers realize the value of these technologies (which it is apparent they are starting to do) the marketers who adopt early will be the ones who benefit from their "gee-whiz" aspect—just like the marketers of seven years ago capitalized on the uniqueness of that "old" Internet standby, the banner ad.

DID YOU EVER THINK YOUR DATA WOULD BE THIS VALUABLE?

That's really the question that must be asked. In creating your multi-million dollar CRM investment, you've developed a goldmine that has helped you build solid rapport with your customers. That goldmine can prove to be the stepping stone to the next generation of customers—those that are purchasing products and service online (and beyond). In turn, the online applications that we have discussed here can give back to you in your offline efforts by providing a complete view of your customers, so that you know what their interests are at any given time, and therefore, can market to them accordingly. Your marketing campaigns can be optimized not only on the Web, but through traditional media as well.

When turning your "brick and mortar" into a "click and mortar," remember that things are different online. Customers may have the same interests, but they have a different way of researching the items that they are interested in. They're more likely to browse at a leisurely pace, for instance, which means that you have a greater chance of getting their attention. Conversely, however, people online are notoriously fickle about the information they receive; if it's not relevant to them, the chances are you'll spend more time annoying them than you will converting them. Which makes the data that you have all the more valuable; the more accurate it is, the greater understanding you have of your customers, the better chance you have of developing relationships that will be long-lasting and beneficial.

The evolution of the information economy resulting in such new paradigms as e-commerce has brought the notion of data transformation into information and knowledge to new levels. The real-time environment of e-commerce entails a constant flow of information rich data which, with the aid of state-of-the-art technology such as data mining and creative business strategy can be utilized to benefit both producers and consumers of goods and services.

REFERENCES

Gormley T .J., Dolberg S., Coles S. (1999). *The Demise of CRM*, Forrester Research, June.

Chapter VII

Improving the Web Experience Through Real-Time Analysis: A Market Basket Approach

by Macromedia

The previous chapter introduced the evolution of the information economy as it addressed the progress of commerce from "brick and mortar" to "click and mortar" corporate initiatives. The key to the success of this process lies in the management of data by transforming it into usable information and applying appropriate business strategy. This chapter provides a natural extension to this topic as it describes the process by which organizations can achieve success on the Internet through the use of data, technology and sound management tactics.

E-commerce vendors face two important challenges: driving up purchases and maintaining customer loyalty. However, only 2.7 percent of browsers buy from any given Web site and only 15 percent of those buyers return to buy again (Forrester Research, Inc.). To succeed, e-marketers must find ways to keep visitors on their sites. They must make the visitors' experience convenient, satisfying and personally relevant. Above all, they must entice Web visitors to come back for more.

To accomplish this, e-commerce vendors must have information. For instance, who is your online audience? What attracts them? What retains them? Are your company's online investments (spending on advertising, e-commerce, site development, etc.) paying off? How can you achieve your company's business objectives through a Web site?

These questions, and more, are becoming increasingly common as the Internet continues to quicken the pace of business around the world. However, many enterprises aren't finding the answers they need. Instead, the tools required to uncover this information either aren't being employed, or are being used at their most basic level.

This means that businesses that want to leverage the Internet still have a long way to go to realize their objectives. Meanwhile, there seems to be a consensus that there are a number of key benefits to replicating marketing practices in e-business, including:

- Increased customer loyalty
- Increased customer stickiness
- Increased impulse purchases
- Increased cross-selling

We will explore a solution available today that software engineers can implement to help e-marketers achieve the benefits of bringing brick-and-mortar marketing to the Internet. It's a technology that extends traditional market basket analysis techniques to the Internet through progressive collaborative filtering techniques and item affinity detection.

AN INTRODUCTION TO INTERNET PERSONALIZATION

The purpose of this chapter is to introduce a new type of Internet personalization, Item Affinity. First, we will introduce the basic concepts surrounding personalization, including traditional rules-based personalization and the more progressive collaborative filtering techniques. Then, we will introduce item affinity personalization and look at the concepts and benefits of market basket analysis, which forms the basis for item affinity recommendations. We will compare the benefits and liabilities inherent to the two approaches, construct likely user scenarios for two Web sites, and then discuss the configurations that must be specified to extend the flexibility of item affinity detection for making meaningful, real-time recommendations in the information-rich environment of the Internet.

Basic Personalization

There are three types of personalization:

- Rules-based personalization
- Collaborative filtering
- Item affinity

We will briefly discuss each here.

At its core, personalization refers to making recommendations based on some event unique to each visitor—whether a purchase, visit to a particular area or some other activity. This is a very familiar concept. For instance, when we go to a grocery store, we might receive a coupon that was triggered by something we purchased. This can be defined as rules-based personalization—that is, a rule exists that says, 'if butter is purchased, offer a coupon for margarine.'

This method of personalization works best in an environment where the number of items offered and the users who purchase them are rather low. Rules also perform well when price points are high or purchasing frequency is low. The reason for this is that when diversity is limited, rules typically continue to apply to specific groups with some margin of success.

Another more intuitive example of personalization is found in the hair styling business. A good stylist can meet with brand new customers and, after looking at their hair and asking a few questions, give those customers hairstyles that are uniquely suited to them. This form of personalization is called intuitive collaborative filtering, since the stylist is basing their recommendation of a preferred style on all of the customers that they have been able to satisfy in the past.

This collaborative filtering model is ideal for use on a Web site by comparing individuals with the peer group that is most similar to them. Then, the Web site can make recommendations that are generated by looking at the actions of that peer group. The result: highly active, intuitive recommendations.

Item affinity is simply the propensity or likelihood of one item to be associated in any way with another item. Our lives are full of such relationships, including adages we use every day—such as milk and cookies, nuts and bolts, and love and marriage. These detail how well human beings understand that certain things naturally seem to go with certain other things.

As it applies to the Web, item affinity allows you to match any product with a list of other products that the user would be most likely to want to purchase. In other words, based on content that the user is currently viewing or has already placed in the shopping cart, the item affinity can recommend products that were also purchased or viewed by other users at the same time that they purchased these products.

However, item affinity isn't concerned with human relationships. If a person could go to a Web site and choose love, item affinity would or wouldn't recommend 'marriage' based on the association between the two over time. How people interact isn't generally a factor in making item affinity recommendations. Think of it this way: If Albert Einstein and Homer Simpson both had a hammer, they'd both be looking for a nail. Item affinity wouldn't have any way of knowing that one is a genius and the other is an oafish cartoon character. The recommendation for the nail would be the result of their mutual affinity for a hammer.

Most important, item affinity is a clever implementation of traditional market basket analysis techniques for the Internet.

Collaborative Filtering Brings New Dimension of Pattern Recognition to Personalization

With collaborative filtering, users are assigned a set of mentors. The mentor pool constantly evolves for any individual user. For instance, the people in that group today might not be there tomorrow, depending on how they relate to you and your behavior in the future. As you change, your mentor group will change as well, becoming more accurate because there is more data available to choose who occupies your mentor groups.

Collaborative filtering brings to the table a dimension of pattern recognition that greatly complements rules. Essentially, rules are based upon strong patterns from the past anticipated as being true again in the future. When the extent of past and obvious patterns has been exhausted, rules are usually left to do their thing on that complement of the marketplace where they have proven themselves—regardless of whether more, new, or better rules are forthcoming.

However, that doesn't mean that there aren't more patterns left in the data, or that new patterns might not emerge in the future. Classic poor marketing acts as if past patterns will be unequivocally true in the future, despite not knowing (or trying to know) anything about how the marketplace or their users might have changed across time.

One last aspect of what collaborative filtering can bring to any business lies in the nature of similarity within populations of human beings. Rules-based applications don't bother to assign any real meaning to their rules—they are simply applied to everyone who qualifies.

Rules can and do work. The challenge is knowing when they are getting a bit rusty, when they are missing large parts of the potential market, and when they are no longer valid. Collaborative filtering provides marketers with several key advantages. Not only is this type of personalization adaptive in real time, which is critical in effectively targeting promotions, it also scales well for a large number of products and users. Finally, there is no other tool available that truly markets to a single person—except, that is, item affinity.

Item Affinity: An Extension to Traditional Market Basket Analysis

Market basket analysis was originally devised for use in grocery stores. The purpose is to count the number of times items occur in the same shopping cart together to construct statistics to tell the tale of the strength and reliability of the item-to-item affinities detected. Market basket analysis counts the number of times every item occurs with every other item (in pairs, triplets, quadruplets, etc.).

Marketers have been relying on market basket analysis to determine what products customers purchase together for years. This methodology works quite well in the three-dimensional world. The classic example is people buying orange juice in conjunction with cough syrup. Without market basket analysis, this would not be an intuitive choice for a product combination.

As with all things analytical, the deeper one delves into the item-to-item space, the less sample size there will be to substantiate the item affinity relationships found. Therefore, there is a limit to the useful statistical data that can be provided by conventional market basket analysis.

While detecting item affinities and making recommendations based on those relationships is the real charter for both market basket analysis and item affinity, the most critical part of exploiting the item affinity dynamic is to configure the recommendation approach in such a way as to take advantage of conventional commerce issues like seasonality, sparse or infrequent purchase patterns, large item inventories, highly diverse price-points, etc. Item affinity can be designed to do this within Internet applications in ways that market basket analysis was not designed.

One Advantage of Market Basket Analysis Over Item Affinity

Conventional market basket analysis has a time-related advantage over item affinity. Because market basket analysis is so time-consuming to perform, there isn't the performance pressure experienced by a real-time recommendation engine. As such, market basket analysis can take as much time as needed to descend the item affinity tree looking for every possible item-to-item combination to detect every possible item affinity rule.

It should be noted that such an approach is forced to take much more of its already protracted analysis cycle deciding which rules, of all the millions of market basket analysis rules generated, truly have an affinity for each other. So the real advantage of market basket analysis over item affinity is the method of delivering recommendations based on the time differential that separates their recommendation window.

This makes all such promotions more bounded by economic security, and yet they clearly run the risk of missing out on promoting certain items whose affinities for each other are driven by temporary fads, specific to a limited geographical area, or unexpected, yet short-term, seasonal consumption patterns.

Item Affinity: Taking the Best of Market Basket Theory to the Internet

As explained previously, item affinity is a refinement of conventional market basket analysis. It is also an astute example of online market basket analysis. This powerful methodology provides Web sites with the valuable data they need to uncover meaningful product combinations. Armed with this information, marketers can more effectively target promotions and perform cross-selling over the Internet.

Item affinity can look at pair associations of items that were purchased, or selected together. Given an item, this approach allows Web sites to then determine which other item is most likely to be purchased at the same time.

This analysis is extremely useful, and can be used in a variety of scenarios. For instance it can be used at point-of-sale for up-sell and cross-sell. It is also adaptable to providing product pair recommendations for banking services, medical treatment combinations, insurance claim combinations, and items bought on a credit card.

Item affinity is particularly effective at recommending products where the purchasing connection between products is not obvious, but is nonetheless very strong. For instance, the beer and diapers example.

How an Implementation of Item Affinity Works in Comparison to Market Basket Analysis

Unlike market basket analysis, item affinity limits itself to pairs, rather than looking at all possible item associations. Yet, by allowing multiple ways to define market baskets and multiple things or events to count, item affinity compensates for the loss of information that comes from not analyzing every possible item combination. This provides Web sites with increased marketing flexibility and computing speed. As a result, Web sites can analyze a more complete spectra of e-commerce events.

This flexibility extends item affinity's recommendation abilities well past market basket analysis, taking the past-purchases-at-the-checkout-counter-only approach into the realm of analyzing item affinity relationships within the full scope of Web-browsing activities. This includes tracking purchases, as well as tracking other events, such as page views critical to an item's purchase and shopping cart adds and drops.

For example, the Macromedia LikeMinds' implementation of item affinity uses a background process called the Accumulator. Through this process, item affinity can be configured with as many ways to define market baskets along with as many events to count as a specific Web application might require to realize their specific business strategy. The Accumulator is the background data processing component of the item affinity engine. This utility runs in the background processing all of the item event data. It writes the results of this data processing, or accumulation, out to a table. The item affinity engine then uses this information to make item affinity recommendations.

When the same flexible approach to defining market baskets is applied to defining which Web events to count, item affinity can address even more complex aspects of commerce, such as using November/December market baskets to make recommendations during a pre-Christmas sale, alternatively using lifetime and session market baskets for recommendations made for infrequently purchased items, and using critical page view counts for making recommendations on items that are more difficult to sell or have never been sold previously without the presence of one or two other item-specific sales.

Using market basket analysis to detect an affinity between items is an approach that is well suited to grocery stores and large retail chains. But for the special problems presented in World Wide Web applications, item affinity capitalizes on sales dynamics inherent to the Internet that affect item affinity in a way that conventional market basket analysis just cannot hope to address.

A Recap of Why Item Affinity is Superior to Market Basket Analysis for Online Marketing

Item affinity has some distinct advantages over conventional market basket analysis. For starters, item affinity can be configured to analyze and

Table 7.1.

Feature Comparisons of Market Basket Analysis and an Implementation of Real-Time Item Affinity

Feature	Conventional MBA	Real-Time Item Affinity
Item affinity coverage	All possible combinations of items	All possible *pairs* of items
Ease of application	Quite cumbersome; an interface between the analysis computer to cash register is required to wed the market basket analysis statistics to the recommendations (and is often absent)	Fast API calls; time is spent making recommendations to Web visitors and not making costly item affinity calculations and repeated database calls
Timing of recommendation	Next visit	Real-time
Multiple basket definition	Lifetime or 'sessionized' market baskets are possible. 'Sessionized'-baskets-only is the norm; counts purchases only	Baskets based on customer lifetime, sessions, months, weeks, females only, males only, income > $50,000/yr only, all are possible within IA
Multiple event counting capability	Items purchased only	Full spectrum of web-events tracking: purchases, shopping cart adds & drops, critical page views, etc.
Efficiency of computations	Days to weeks to complete, with recommendations made only at the end of the checkout cycle (coupons given out only after current payment is made)	Analysis runs in the background and recommendations are presented in real time, while the customer is still engaged on the site
Ideal use profiles	Best for high volume sites or stores, with high frequency items	Custom configuration for all levels of sales volume and frequency
Item affinity rules complexity	The "as deep as it goes" approach makes most item affinity rules incomprehensible	Pair-wise rules applied in real time make item affinity rules interpretation moot

then make recommendations from the results of multiple market baskets, such as lifetime, monthly and specific-seasonal baskets. This is in contrast to merely counting the items that occur at the checkout station together in the same shopping cart.

Item affinity can be configured to count transactions other than mere purchases. For instance, item affinity can count elements that comprise the bulk of e-commerce transactions—such as shopping cart adds or drops or critical page views—and then convey strong item affinity dynamics of their own. Market basket analysis doesn't have this capability.

Item affinity is capable of making recommendations on the basis of many states of shared item space—what is placed in the cart at any point in time, the full contents of a shopping cart at any point in time, what has ever resided in the same shopping regardless of lack of purchase, or items that exist in the cart only at checkout time.

While market basket analysis can be thought of as detecting item affinities as measured only at checkout time and then only by counting actual purchases, item affinity should be thought of as detecting item affinities as they exist at any time during a Web visitor's lifetime—not just at checkout time.

In this way, item affinity is seen as a more full-purpose item affinity recommendation engine than market basket analysis. It also provides the flexibility and ease of use tailored to transactions seen on a wide variety of Web sites, and is specifically designed for transaction types and frequencies more typical to e-commerce applications than for brick-and-mortar retail outlets.

A MORE DETAILED DESCRIPTION OF ITEM AFFINITY

Counting Basics—How Item Affinity Goes About Its Tasks

Let's look into more details of the differences between market basket analysis and item affinity—as shown in Table 7.1 above—through multiple baskets and expanding events.

Multiple Baskets: Telling Item Affinity How to Count by Compressing Time

The grocery business is designed around point-of-purchase marketing dynamics done amid a myriad of advertising stands, in a sea of competition for the best shelf-space, and massive marketing programs including both coupons and vouchers for free products of the competitors of your current purchases. Thus, for the grocer, deciding 'how' to count is cut and dried.

While counting all of the purchases a customer has ever made in their lifetime could yield some interesting results (considering the user's lifetime to be the market basket definition in this case), many grocers have seen that their real bread-and-butter is in boosting daily cross-sales. For Internet applications, the concept of defining multiple market baskets becomes critical to the level of performance the item affinity recommendations can make.

Think of each market basket definition as a set of unique keys that tell item affinity how to classify whether items have ever shared 'the item affinity space,' be it in a singular shopping cart or across that user's entire customer lifetime. On the Internet, item affinity can track each user's lifetime purchases as one market basket and can also track them according to their minute-to-minute Internet browsing. While both these market basket classifications measure the same behavior, they will yield radically different counts for the different market baskets' shared item space.

Another way to think of why one might want to define multiple market baskets is as a strategy for controlling time. While a business can control many aspects of their own destiny, how often and how frequently customers make their inquiries and purchases is generally not one of them. This is particularly true on the Internet, when a person can quickly and with minimal effort visit a competing site. As a result, the time between purchases—or, in the case of content-only sites, detailed views—is a critical aspect of any sales analysis, and for item affinity analysis this is particularly true. Therefore, without the ability to define multiple ways to count, item affinity would not be able to detect the sort of item affinity dynamics common to and specifically true of Internet applications.

A business that has large yet infrequent purchases might not be well suited to limiting its item affinity analysis to rigorously defined Internet sessions only, since each item is usually purchased alone. There would be very little item affinity to exploit. It would be applied to detecting similarities where there is little to no item affinity to be found. However, if the definition of the market basket were broadened a bit, by substituting an Internet session market basket with a daily or even broader market basket, item affinities that were not detectable in an Internet session market baskets begin to surface.

Similarly, a business that has frequent and regular purchases might be best served by combining the individual, multiple sessions that occur for a user in a month into monthly market baskets, since the marketing promotions are changed monthly.

Multiple Events: Telling Item Affinity What to Count By Expanding Events

Imagine that the grocer somehow seems to know all the items that you even remotely considered while you shopped, if even quite briefly or without much serious consideration. Then, they could factor that information into a conventional market basket analysis for making recommendations at the checkout counter based on things you almost put into your shopping cart.

That is exactly what item affinity does with its feature for specifying multiple 'events' to count. Each Internet event conveys some aspect of the item affinity dynamic a marketer seeks to identify and then uses to make eventual recommendations.

By allowing for the definition of multiple ways to count, as well as multiple definitions of what to count, item affinity has adapted the tenets of market basket analysis to a more information-rich environment—such as the Internet—and tailored it to the unique world of real-time recommendations.

Another reason why a marketer would want to define multiple events to count is as a strategy for exploiting the diversity of one's own product offerings. The quantity and frequency of purchases is a critical aspect of any sales analysis. Without the ability to define multiple events to count, item affinity would be severely limited by the sparseness of purchases relative to the rest of the Internet traffic it sees. This would deny item affinity the opportunity to factor in related events, such as critical page views or shopping cart adds, and it would therefore miss many of the item affinity dynamics that are possible to detect within e-commerce applications.

ITEM AFFINITY IN THE REAL WORLD

In order to see how item affinity (with collaborative filtering as discussed earlier) works in the real world, we'll look at four probable implementations. The software used in the examples is Macromedia LikeMinds, a real-time, personalization solution that contains both item affinity and collaborative filtering capabilities.

Gift Recommender

A Web site selling gifts wants to institute a recommendation stream for visitors to their site. The complexity here is that the person is not buying items for themselves, but for another person. In that context, using that user's past purchases as a barometer for their similarity to other users (their eventual mentors) would be a bad source for gifts for someone else.

Solution

- Use the item affinity to define several different baskets of past gift buying history (a lifetime view of gift purchases, a Christmas view, an Easter view, a seasonal view, etc.). This will compile all shared items in the various 'baskets,' making sure that the item affinity engine is configured to count gift purchases, thereby allowing the eventual recommendations to fit into the seasonal context that many gifts fall into. (This does not include, of course, birthdays, housewarmings, etc.)

Benefits

- Recommendations are based on purchases the visitor indicates they did not purchase for themselves, usually indicative of a gift for someone else.
- Recommendations are based on past gift purchases across typical gift-exchange seasons.

Help Desk

A software company wants to better support its users and the help that is extended to them online, instead of opting for spending more resources on the more expensive conduit of providing technical assistance over the phone.

Solution

Configure the items to be pages in the online help database and then configure the item affinity engine to track the pages that users go to for help. The item affinity engine can then be used in two ways:

- *Offline analytics*: roll out in a test environment where the support and documentation analysts can see right in front of them which pages occur together most often, allowing them insight into which pages and topical matters are apparently the most poorly designed, or areas of help that might indicate areas of typical user confusion
- *Online recommendation*: make 'help page' recommendations to the user of the form "...other users in your straits found information on the following pages to be of help to them..."

Benefits

- Gives insight into areas of user confusion that can improve the product.
- Allows for proactive changes in documentation based on user history and patterns instead of guessing.
- Reduces the overall cost of user support when it can act as an enhance-

ment, or even wholesale replacement, for expensive direct technical support.

CONCLUSION

Item affinity doesn't pretend to be a replacement for traditional market basket analysis. Rather, it is simply an extension, a method that opens the online world to the same marketing intelligence that market basket analysis has already provided to brick-and-mortar businesses. By employing item affinity techniques, which deliver trustworthy recommendations for products and services, enterprises can convert Web surfers into loyal customers. This also means that sites with item affinity capabilities—in addition to collaborative filtering techniques—will capture additional wallet share from online customers.

Item affinity is the best marketing tool when:
- A Web site visitor has little or no history in the host site's database.
- A Web site wants to retrieve items that are strongly associated with other items.
- A Web site wants to cross-sell and up-sell.

Item affinity is an ideal marketing tool, serving the marketing needs of e-commerce sites, as well as the needs of content-oriented and other sites. And, unlike rules-based personalization, engineers don't have to write—or continually update—rules. In addition, item affinity surpasses collaborative filtering by making recommendations to new users when no behavioral data exists.

Clearly, technical professionals need to take a close look at the available options, selecting only those that will further their company's Web site objectives, while providing them with the ease of use and flexibility they will require as the Internet continues to evolve.

Chapter VIII

Bringing It All Together (Data Mining on an Enterprise Level)

Up to now we have presented the fundamental building blocks to understanding the concept of data mining and addressed the prevailing applications within the corporate environment including both the "brick and mortar" style and e-commerce spectrums. The process does not stop here however. In order to implement mining on an enterprise basis, firms must overcome some potentially serious obstacles and address key issues.

The more complex nature of data mining generally limits its use to a smaller population of individuals in a given firm, (although this is not always the case). Because of this, a common drawback to the process of effective Mining is the communication of value-added model results to corresponding users of this information. Just as there exists a gap between IT personnel, (those who know the technical side of systems) and the business user, (those who require IT systems to help solve their problems), there also exists a communication gap between the "data miners" and those who need to apply the resulting models to help solve their business problem.

Other issues which must be considered before implementing an organization wide mining approach entails the development of total mining solutions instead of limiting applications to a few business problems. Decision makers must also avoid the trap of relying too heavily on mining results and must remember that these models are not crystal ball providers of perfect knowledge. Because of this, they must therefore monitor actual business performance against projected measures to maintain model effectiveness and accuracy.

This chapter will provide some insights on how to address these key issues in order to more fully capture the added value that mining technology offers to the bottom line of the firm. It will then reintroduce the mining solution space within the realm of business intelligence technology and the corporate IT system to solidify how the technologies can be utilized as a "business intelligence system."

THE GAP PROBLEMS:
(Communication and Knowledge)

A key term to keep in mind refers to the "communication and knowledge gap". Data mining personnel generally include sophisticated analysts, many times involving Ph.D. level statisticians, mathematicians and econometricians. This of course is the highest end of the spectrum; However the majority of proficient miners have a good sense of statistics that enable them to create credible, reliable models. This poses a problem, since many decision makers don't have the specialized expertise nor the time to fully understand the mining process or how to effectively utilize corresponding models. What you have then is the potential for a separation of the business user (those who fully understand the business application) and the miners (those who are one step removed from the real-time environment and are more numbers orientated). This separation could result in deterioration in the overall mining process. The process here not only refers to creating models but effectively implementing their results to enhance firm productivity. The specialized personnel creating corresponding models can sometimes miss critical information that may impact an application. So what seems to be a robust model (statistically sound result), may be too far removed from reality to provide a value-added solution for the business population.

Another problem regarding data mining deployment involves ineffective implementation of value-added mining results to the proper users. Model forecasts, profiles and segmentation results are often buried in the analytical zones of a given enterprise. For example, analysts may create reports and conduct presentations about what mining results imply to business strategy but decision makers fail to correctly implement the process that is required to achieve results. In other words, "the model looks fine but we'll stick with our way of making decisions." This may be a function of either not trusting the mining analysis or not fully understanding the process. Regardless of the source of rejection, the bottom line remains that these limitations are a result of a knowledge and communication gap between the mining and non-mining community.

So What is the Answer?

Data mining technology enables users/analysts to identify relationships among variables in their data that pertain to an application corresponding to a given functional area in an organization. It is being incorporated more and more by firms across industry sectors as the availability and access to data has been enhanced and the technology itself has become more user-friendly. *The key to using this potentially powerful technology to one's greatest benefit revolves around connecting qualified miners with the real business process to create truly credible results and effectively communicate these results to the appropriate information consumers.* This issue is complex and concrete answers are difficult to provide, however the following sections in this chapter regarding variance reporting and cross functional communication, along with the evolution of data mining and the employee of the future in Chapter 9, offer some indirect solutions to closing the communication and knowledge gap.

STEPS TO ACHIEVING A TOTAL SOLUTION WITH MINING

One Model Rarely Captures an Entire Business Solution: (A Human Resource Application)

When attempting to produce a truly value-added business model, the miner must adopt the process described in Chapter 3 of this book, which addresses the steps to success or rules of thumb to follow in order to achieve reliable mining results. The result of this process generally does not entail an end all, generic, all encompassing model, but rather a system of models that answer particular business level questions. This requires effective communication between the business user who is asking the question and the miner who will attempt to provide an answer.

For example, in a human resource application, the solution may require an employee attrition analysis. In other words, business analysts wish to quantitatively examine trends regarding the outflow of employees of their organization. Given the recent tight demand for labor in the US and increasing demand for IT skills, this topic has become a source of concern for many organizations. At first glance, the solution appears to be one-dimensional, where a general cross-sectional analysis may suffice. In reality however, the complete solution will entail a number of approaches which address a multidimensional space. The initial process may include a regression or neural net time series analysis examining the numbers of employees who have left an organization (target), which may incorporate such driving variables as macro economic indicators including the nations unemployment rate and economic growth rates, or more micro variables unique to the firms such as number of employees eligible for retirement (drivers). However the entire solution may not rest with this application. Managers are not only interested in how many people have left their firm but why. Knowing why employees are leaving enables managers to better control the firms' attrition rate. Once models have identified the critical factors driving attrition, managers can implement policies (address those factors that cause attrition) to correct the problem.

To answer the why question, the miner can perform a cross-sectional analysis involving a sample of employees with corresponding descriptive fields (job and employee profiles) along with resulting indicators measuring whether the person is currently with the firm or whether they have left. A neural network, logit regression or even segmentation methodology should be able to identify how various profile aspects may have influenced a person's activity to stay or leave.

The process may not end at this stage. To more fully understand employee activities, analysts may seek to create employee performance models (e.g., mine those factors that impact employee activity rates), or they may seek to identify driving factors behind why workers decide to retire. In essence, the thorough and value-added mining approach should not rely on "the all-encompassing model" but rather on a group of models that answers a particular question. This issue is not restricted to human resources but is essential to most mining applications. The user/ miner must consider different angles that encompass the given task. For advertising effectiveness, the miner must consider whether to construct more macro-focused models that analyze the affects advertising expenditure have on overall market share. They may then want to consider how different types of advertising, (e.g., print, media) impact market share, or they may want to analyze how advertising and promotions impact a particular brand. Insurance companies may want to analyze why certain policies have higher claim rates. The mining process may not only include a claims analysis but a claim profitability analysis.

Other mining applications include cost or profit models which require the analyst to identify the relevant level of detail of data to incorporate in the model (e.g., costs or profits according to products, product lines, branches or regions). Once this process has been completed, the solution should become a greater value added to decision makers. Systems of models that more accurately answer a number of questions of an overall solution more adequately increase the knowledge of the decision makers.

Don't Adopt Blind Adherence to Existing Models

Even the best mining solutions are mere quantitative models that identify statistically significant relationships between variables over historical data. These solutions serve as guides to users to help them identify patterns between explanatory and target variables to more accurately predict the outcomes in variables given a set of expected inputs. Some models are extremely accurate while others offer more ball park estimations. Some maintain a credible accuracy over an extended period of time while others quickly lose their explanatory accurateness over the short term.

The key to effective utilization of mining analysis is to close the communication and knowledge gap between miners and business users. Miners generally have a feel of the accuracy level or credibility of corresponding models, which should be communicated to the model consuming audience. This avoids the potential pitfall of blind adherence to model output. The process does not rest on the shoulders of the mining community alone. The communication process is a two-way street and requires the user audience to voice dismay with model performance when variances become extreme or, in other words, the reliability of the model is seriously in question.

Inventory managers in a supply chain management environment must communicate noticeable increases in demand forecast variances that result in nonproductive inventory management processes. For example, forecasting models that provide demand forecasts for products enable supply chain managers to cut down on wasted over supplies of inventories (warehousing costs) or bottlenecks in the production processes, (e.g., labor shortages or over utilization of machinery). Demand forecasting models may provide accurate schedules over a period of time but this may not be the case over an extended period. It is necessary to continuously monitor the variances between what models have predicted and what actually transpired. When variances become too extreme, the models must be re-optimized.

MODEL OPTIMIZATION AND AN INTRODUCTION TO VARIANCE (Making Sure Models Are Capturing The Business Process)

This topic plays an essential role in the world of valued-added data mining. Generally, mining models are only effective if they identify relationships in data that reflect the underpinnings of a particular business environment. In other words, the data that is examined by the various mining techniques has to be an accurate representation of current business drivers. The topic relates back to the previous chapter regarding the steps to effective mining. If you mine data that is out of date, or are not representative of your current business environment, your results will provide an inaccurate picture of what's driving your business application. So even if a model appears to be robust in identifying relationships, it is only good if it provides insight against what is happening today and tomorrow. Hence, robust models are those that result in small variances between what mining applications imply and what actually occurs in day to day operations.

This topic is increasingly becoming the focus of mining efforts as the optimization process has become more dynamic. One of the primary reasons for this involves the progression of the information economy where e-business has altered the state of the old brick and mortar style organization, (see Chapter 6). Issues such as the changing preferences of customers and competitive strategies by corporations across industry sectors are constantly pushing the envelope of business operations.

Optimization must be kept in context of the application at hand. Some applications involve a more static analytical environment such as seasonality patterns in demand forecasting, advertising on brand awareness or trends in employee attrition. Some of these more static, less volatile environments, sometimes only require a semi-annual re-optimization of mining models. However, as stated above, the information economy has introduced not only a more dynamic nature to business practice but also some Information/e-business specific type of applications. One of these entails the widely cited CRM application.

CRM Revisited (A Dynamic Mining Environment)

Customer relationship management is a dynamic process by which firms seek to retain valued customers and attract new ones. Mining applications such as profiling techniques help decision-makers identify clients and per-spective clients that may respond to products, campaigns or services. These profiling models are under constant scrutiny as to their optimized effectiveness as businesses must adjust operations to accommodate new and different consumers and consumer preferences. Therefore mining models require a more frequent fine-tuning since the process of customer responsiveness is a highly volatile application. In other words, profiling models should be readily monitored as to their effectiveness in capturing the likely habits of particular customers. This generally requires a higher frequency of model regeneration or optimization. For a more thorough explanation of this topic see Chapter 6.

Other Factors that Promote a Dynamic Business Environment: Competitive Forces in Industry (GAME Theory)

Advanced computer processing capabilities and corresponding analytical techniques have brought about methodologies in business strategy such as game theory. This process involves an analytical approach by corporate decision-makers that actually takes into account the probabilistic response of competitors to a company's strategic initiatives, (e.g., price leadership, or product differentiation strategies). In other words, before companies decide to raise prices they may run simulations on what to expect from competitors as a reaction. This type of dynamic decision making throughout the world of commerce adds to the changing face of business drivers and requires a constant optimization of analytical/mining models in organizations across industry sectors. In essence, the faster pace of the information economy with the corresponding explosion of data and analytical technology affects all firms. As a result, many of them are implementing "state of the art" processes to better compete in the market place. This is promoting more frequent and timely business optimization strategies by a greater number of firms in all industries which adds to the dynamic character of commerce today.

The Changing Structure of the Economy and Macro Model Optimization

This notion of an increasing need to optimize because of the changing state of the information economy is clearly depicted in the case of macroeconomic models which are generally classified as econometric models, (discussed in Chapter 2). These models entail a multivariate approach that incorporates a number of variables in the attempt to explain and predict changes in inflation, and economic growth for example. These complex models often incorporate historical data that extend well into the past. Recently however, economic anomalies such as the low level of unemployment, rising economic growth rates and a lack of traditional inflationary influences, which many attribute to the information economy (Kudyba, 1998), have caused many top analysts to re-optimize their models in order to more accurately describe the cause and effect nature of macroeconomic variables. More modern models may only include historical data back to 1995, which is more representative of this newer economy.

Variance Analysis Revisited

The changing face of business in the new information age has resulted in a constant change in business strategy from activities involving the production of goods and services, their distribution and pricing and advertising, to compete, thrive and survive in the market place. Competitors' activity can change from price follower to leader, new competitors can appear in a moments notice through partnership, merger or acquisition.

So what does this all mean to the world of data mining? It means that modelers and those who rely on models must continuously monitor the effectiveness and accuracy of these models and analysis. This process entails a variance analysis by decision makers throughout a given enterprise. In other words, information consumers must examine the difference between what is expected in the market place, (e.g., what data mining models and business managers had projected) and what is actually happening in the real world. Some common examples include:

1) Did price elasticity models hold true as they were projected? (Did product sales increase according to what models had projected price discounts would generate?)
2) Did marketing or advertising campaigns or expenditures result in projected sales increases?
3) Did changes in specified manufacturing processes or parts suppliers result in the reduction in defects as anticipated?
4) Did customer relationship management strategies reduce customer churn or increase product sales?

The above information is critical to data mining analysis and effective implementation of business strategy. In fact, this topic is not limited to the data mining space but is an integral part in the realm of business intelligence. Data mining provides the high end analytics, which may guide business policy. OLAP also plays a role in helping decision makers discover important occurrences throughout a given enterprise through navigation of vast amounts of aggregated data in a cube (see Chapter 1). The accuracy of corresponding business policies which evolve from business intelligence is also imbedded in the BI reporting spectrum. It is the query and reporting and OLAP space that can provide the mechanism to help identify when business policies become ineffective.

Feedback from Functional Areas

Projections of mining analysis and business policy that are reported to corresponding functional areas many times incorporate elements across functional areas. For example, the widely cited CRM application many times involves activities from marketing departments, product development, sales, services and of course the IT infrastructure. Mining applications such as customer profiling or marketing effectiveness uncover the relationships between customer activity measures and corresponding products and services. Effective mining models should be able to uncover a more accurate system that identifies which products and services to offer to particular clients and potentially by which particular methodology (Web site/customer service contact). These processes should result in such outcomes as:

1) Better customer retention (less churn)
2) Increased customer activity rates (increased purchases of goods and services)

The point to stress above involves the assertion *should result*. Projected outcomes many times do not meet expectations, and it is this issue that must be communicated to the appropriate functional areas and ultimately back to data miners. Reasons behind the ineffectiveness of mining results may include the omission of important business drivers for a particular application, inaccurate data sources, bad data or just a changing character of the business environment.

Regardless of the reasoning, the point remains that the variances between projections and true business activity must be monitored and reported to all those involved. This point can be illustrated by the example when a marketing department receives reports that sales are slumping which may indicate poor marketing strategies. However if sales were integral to a CRM strategy, the problem could involve a number of other variables, (e.g., poor pricing, poor sales force tactics, ineffective customer service contacts). Therefore, breakdowns in business strategy should be communicated to the data mining area so they can trouble shoot the sources of variance by re-optimizing models. The re-optimization process may include the addition of new variables to the application or analyzing new business sectors by creating new models.

Communication of the business process to all appropriate decision makers is essential to maintaining and enhancing corporate operations across industry sectors. This communication can be facilitated by the query and reporting and OLAP space of the business intelligence continuum. Variance dimensions can be displayed via these methodologies to raise the awareness of the success or failure of business strategies. Therefore it is important to keep in mind that the entire BI spectrum (data extraction, reporting, OLAP and mining) plays an essential role in facilitating the communication of value added information throughout a given enterprise and therefore may lead to greater efficiency, productivity and profitability for the corresponding firm (Tapscott, 1999).

An overall model (Figures 8.1 to 8.8) which encompasses the BI spectrum of complementary technologies is illustrated below. Generally the scenario depicted involves the incorporation of reporting technology that has extracted data from a corresponding repository (warehouse or mart) and has been distributed and reported to appropriate users. The next step involves the creation of an OLAP Cube (Figure 8.2) that contains multidimensional business data which enables analysts to quickly slice and dice and filter variables to help answer business questions. The final stage depicts two levels of data mining, the first, which illustrates a segmentation application and the second a neural network application that provides a high-end statistical and quantitative analysis of a particular business problem.

Figure 8.1 illustrates a standardized report that quickly informs a large number of users throughout an organization of the status of a functional area:

Figure 8.1.

Financial Report for Company XYZ (Quarter 3, 1998)

Date	Product Lines	Gross Revenue	Profit	% Change from Prev.
Qtr 1 1998	Apparel	$22,245,000	$2,114,000	NA
Qtr 2 1998	Apparel	$22,980,000	$2,250,000	6.4%
Qtr 3 1998	Apparel	$20,138,000	$1,990,000	(-11.5%)

The above report indicates a significant deterioration in financial performance in the apparel line for Company XYZ in the third quarter.

An OLAP Cube depicting corresponding dimensions for XYZ Sales is provided in Figure 8.2.

Figure 8.2.

Time	Channel	Product Lines	Region	Activity Measure
Monthly	In Store	Men's Apparel	East Coast	Gross Sales
Quarterly	Mail Order	Women's Apparel	West Coast	Gross Margin
			Central	Units Sold
			N. America	Returns

The corresponding user can navigate through the cube to narrow down the potential root of the drop off in company performance indicated in the report. After slicing and dicing and filtering on variables, the user/analyst can quickly identify a significant increase in overall product returns (both Men's and Women's Apparel) in only the Mail Order Channel over the last quarter.

Figure 8.3.

Time	Channel	Apparel	North America	Returns
	In Store		Mail Order	Channel
Q2 1998	15,250		8,000	23,250
Q3 1998	16,500		25,000	41,500

Returns on in-store purchases have maintained rates consistent with normal retail activity.

After brainstorming a bit, management had revealed that a new, near fully automated call center system had been implemented to handle all out of store (mail order) issues during the second quarter of 1998.

After an initial investigation it was apparent that the system had resulted in a significant amount of hang-ups or unfulfilled customer responses. In order to determine what was causing this inefficiency, the company decided to utilize data mining techniques to uncover significant patterns in call center activities. The first application was to apply a segmentation approach to determine the probability of whether a person would hang up before receiving answers to their questions.

Data to be analyzed included a sample of phone calls that involved both full-serviced customers (e.g., no hang-ups) and those that resulted in hang-ups. The variables included:

Variable Name:	*Variable Format:*
Customer Identifier	Numeric (ID no.)
Primary Language (English/Non English) (**Driver**)	Text (English/Non English)
Gender of Customer (**Driver**)	Text (Male/Female)
Length of Time on Hold (**Driver**)	Numeric (seconds)
Ranking of Customer Service Rep. (**Driver**)	Numeric (1 least – 5 best)
Whether the Person Hung Up or Not (**Target**)	Numeric (1 yes – 0 No)

Figure 8.4.

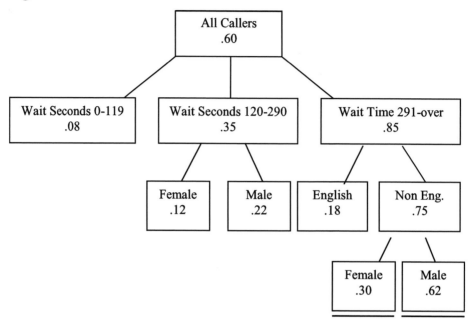

The sample included several thousand phone calls along with above referenced variables. The segmentation analysis produced the following results illustrating how important the variables were in explaining the probability a person would hang up before their issue was resolved (Figure 8.4).

It is evident that the higher propensity to hang-up was a result of individuals with primary language as non English, who were male and were put on hold for more than four minutes.

The same data was then applied to a neural network mining methodology which resulted in the following cross-sections which depict how the drivers correspond with the target (Figures 8.5 to 8.8).

The quantitative impact of the corresponding customer service representative qualification and probability of hang-ups is clearly depicted in Figure 8.5 where the higher the ranking refers to the more well-trained rep.

The neural net model also quantifies the entire variable of seconds waited and resulting hang-up probability (Figure 8.6).

With this model the user can perform a sensitivity analysis and see how the probability of whether a person hangs-up changes as driving variables change since the resulting model includes the multivariate quantitative relationships between variables (regression beta equivalent).

Figure 8.5.

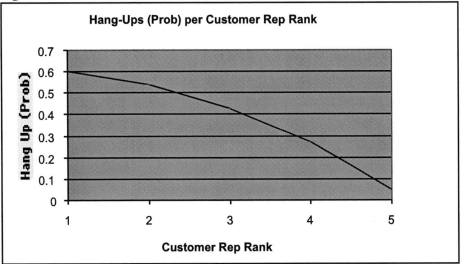

Figure 8.6.

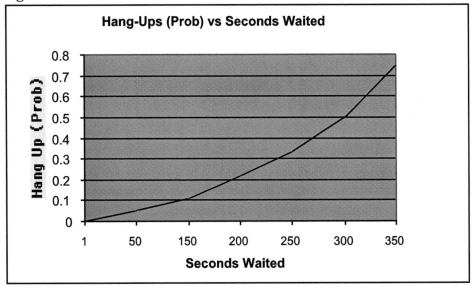

Finally the resulting neural net algorithm can be used to identify the likely hood of hang-ups for customers who have not yet called in. This is done by applying the corresponding customer information (people who purchased apparel through mail order) to the model which will calculate the probability of future hang-ups.

To rectify the problem of the new call center system, which has resulted in a dramatic increase in customer returns, managers can take the following strategic actions:

Figures 8.7 & 8.8. The impacts of categorical variables (gender and primary language) are depicted.

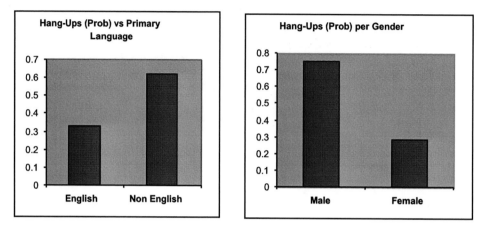

Generally, management has no control over the gender of a customer but can enhance the system by providing more Non-English speaking support functions. It can also implement "red flag" measures to reduce the amount of time people are put on hold under the critical time threshold, (e.g., less than five minutes). Finally, management can better train customer service reps to ensure more effective handling of customer issues.

These policies should result in a more effective call center system that better facilitates customer issues (e.g., wrong sizes in apparel) that should result in reduced product returns. Management can build off this BI analysis by keeping a closer eye on call center effectiveness in the future. This can be done by creating call center OLAP cubes or incorporating call center dimensions in existing cubes so analysts and decision makers can quickly view the effectiveness of this call center/CRM system. Finally, complementary technology such as intranets, Web-enabled OLAP or reporting software can proliferate the information to corresponding users.

THE DATA MINING SOLUTION WITHIN THE BI SPECTRUM AND INTEGRATION WITH OTHER IT COMPONENTS

The process of constructing an optimized mining analysis in the directed mining spectrum (e.g., segmentation, neural nets and regression), can be a cumbersome and time consuming task. The process many times entails gathering data of corresponding variables, applying the appropriate methodology and then optimizing the analysis by adding or dropping existing information.

Streamlining the Mining Process with Data Extraction Technology

The somewhat cumbersome process mentioned above can be improved with the implementation of hardware and software available in the market today. Many mining applications, as complex as they may initially seem, become routine once the process has been defined. Today's query and extraction software has the capabilities of accessing appropriate data in order to conduct a mining analysis. For example, once the initial process of constructing a value added, robust model has been completed, analysts, with the use of contemporary extraction technology, can retrieve corresponding variables (important demographics over a corresponding time period, in the appropriate format), which begins to minimize the massaging or optimizing task mentioned above. Today's IT systems can help facilitate a more routine process to the often complex task of mining.

For example, CRM applications generally incorporate a host of demographic, descriptive drivers that describe a particular customer activity rate, (e.g., cancellation, response, purchase). The initial process of mining the appropriate information is a time consuming task as analysts churn through massive volumes of data using such methodologies as clustering, segmentation, neural nets or regression to come up with the best statistical story behind the chosen analysis. Once the process has been defined, (which variables and in what format provide the story behind customer activity) query and extraction technology can help streamline it in the future.

Preliminary Analysis with OLAP to Fine Tune the Mining Application

Other aspects of the business intelligence spectrum can also mitigate the complex task and augment the process of data mining. As was mentioned early in this book, OLAP can provide a significant value added as a first-cut analysis for high-end mining. Well-structured, multi-dimensional cubes of data enable users to quickly and easily slice, dice and filter through a vast amount of pertinent aggregated information. Miners can sometimes gain leverage from this software to simplify the mining process by navigating through a cube to identify sectors of interest regarding a given application. For example, cube navigation (slicing and dicing) can quickly give analysts insights on particular segments of their data that should more rigorously be analyzed, (e.g., particular demographic variables of clients activity in a CRM application). Instead of having to mine through the sometimes vast terabytes of data in a data warehouse, miners can now fine-tune the analysis to particular sectors and categories.

Of course this process is not without its limitations since data within a cube is at the aggregate level and sometimes does not contain the missing important variables that provide the real value added to robust mining models. Despite these limitations, OLAP can no doubt provide a complement to a mining analysis by depicting a general direction in which to proceed.

Putting It All Together

The spectrum of business intelligence technology (data extraction and reporting, OLAP and mining software) in conjunction with essential complementary technology, (P/Cs, servers, telecomm, Internet and Internet-related) come together to create a corporate IT system (Shapiro, 2000). The process of utilizing the business intelligence space within this spectrum to promote the generation of productivity enhancing strategies involves the following general outline:

1) Extracting appropriate data from corresponding storage facilities to create OLAP cubes which provide the first cut to data analysis, (e.g., provide the user with insights on answering a number of business related scenarios and enlightens them on particular applications that need to be more closely examined by data mining methodology).

Once this process has provided a more focused direction regarding a particular application:

2) The mining procedure requires the process of extracting and massaging data on various variables to apply corresponding methodologies (e.g., segmentation, regression, neural networks).

When the above procedure is fine tuned, the data extraction and massaging process can be done in a more routine manner involving:

3) Query and extraction technology that access data located in single or multiple locations, (e.g., one warehouse or numerous data marts) that retrieve data in appropriate formats for further analysis.

The final step then involves the continuous loop of the business intelligence process, that is:

- Reporting value-added information (mining or OLAP analysis results) throughout the corresponding functional areas of a corporate enterprise.
- Monitoring the accuracy of these analytical mechanisms, obtaining

feedback from business users on cube and mining model effectiveness (variance).

- Re-optimizing OLAP and mining and proliferate the information throughout the firm.

The last section of this chapter provides an illustration of the combination of business intelligence technology and complementary technologies that comprise the corporate information system along with some essential issues to consider when attempting to promote productivity in a given firm.

USING IT TO SURVIVE IN THE INFORMATION AGE

Figure 8.9 illustrates an organizational structure of the key information technological applications that are essential to not only achieving a competitive edge but surviving in today's information economy by operating as efficiently and productively as possible. The diagram brings all the attributes previously addressed in this analysis together into a coherent model. Of course this only suggests a general shell of a mechanism to achieve efficiency and does not include the micro details embedded in many of these applications such as software specific technology, or which IT vendors to use, companies to partner with, and specific functions to outsource. The list goes on and on and involves the managerial chemistry of the organization.

Detailed applications involve internal software systems of standard design permitting internal and external communication and integration with complementary technologies internally and with business affiliates. This leads to:

1) Increased communication and information flow.
2) Reduced uncertainty of business drivers.
3) Increased understanding of business and industry processes leading to greater efficiency.
4) Corporate strategies which may include partnerships, outsourcing or merger/acquisition to promote synergy.

The above procedure must be accompanied by effective complementary information technology, which enables various functional areas of a firm to communicate within the firm and with outside sources. E-mail, intranets, LANs and WANs, in conjunction with integrated standard software facilitates information flow within the organization. E-mail, extranets and the Internet enable the corporation to communicate with suppliers, partners and

Figure 8.9.

Model of Key Elements Essential to Productivity Enhancing IT Applications

Information Input → (Transactional/Demographic)
⇓

Data Warehouse/Marts → (Storage Facility)
⇓

Internal Communication   **External Communication**
(e-mail, Intranets, LANS)   **(Customers, Partners, Suppliers)**
                                       (Internet, Extranets)

Extraction, Query and Reporting→ (Raw Data in Usable Format)
⇓

(On Line Analytical Processing)→ (Create Accessible Multidimensional
                                       Cube of Value Added Information)
⇓

Data Mining→ (Identifying Cause and Effect Relationships,
Forecasting Business Drivers)

↑ Loop Back to Business Users with Accurate Models ↑
↑ Explaining Business Drivers ↑

customers outside the organization, which permits companies to outsource procedures to specialists, take advantage of the most efficient suppliers, distribute their product in the most effective way, and identify consumer needs more accurately. Technology is the main driver to this process however an essential ingredient to increasing productivity requires skilled labor according to area specialty that is able to communicate across functional areas within the firm.

REFERENCES

Kudyba, Stephan (1998). Rising Commodities and Higher Inflation, *Futures Magazine*, Nov.

Shapiro, Carl and Varian, Hal (1999). *Information Rules: A Strategic Guide to the Network Economy,* Harvard Business School Press, Boston.

Tapscott, Don (1999). *Creating Value in the Network Economy*, Harvard Business School Press, Boston.

Chapter IX

What the Future Holds for Data Mining

Predicting the future is always a difficult task, of course that depends on how far into the future one attempts to delve. With regard to data mining, there's no doubt the future should entail some interesting new applications that seek to enhance the process of discovering patterns and relationships existing between variables underpinning a given business application. This chapter seeks to enlighten the reader with regards to "what's in the pipeline" for the coming years in the world of data mining.

This topic can be broken down into two major components which include:

1) Innovations in statistics and algorithms that will provide new revelations to the world of mining.
2) Innovations in overall information technology that will augment the current functionality of mining methodology.

This chapter will emphasize the second point mentioned above as the area for the greatest potential for mining enhancements over the next year or so.

A QUICK WORD ON INNOVATIONS IN ALGORITHMS

In the preceding chapters we addressed the evolution of data mining and referred to the core of this methodology as being grounded on econometric modeling, the focal point of which involves the application of regression techniques. Probably, one of the main innovations over the past 5 to 10 years has been the implementation of neural network technology to the world of data mining. I use the terminology "implementation" as opposed to invention since the neural network methodology has been in existence for well over 10 years. It has only been over the past few years or so that many miners/modelers have come to view neural networks as an acceptable methodology to analyze data, and there still is a sector of the mining population that continues to question the validity of this methodology.

Innovations in statistics and algorithms probably aren't the root for enhancements in the world of mining over the medium term but rather the source of true enhancements lie in the innovation of complimentary technology along with the flexible application of current data mining techniques. For example, the evolution of CRM as a driving business strategy has incorporated the use of regression and neural networks along with segmentation and classification methodologies to conduct customer profiling. The underlying algorithms or approaches are not new but the implementations of such are.

THE EVOLUTION OF E-BUSINESS AND NEW DATA MINING

Current mining approaches applied to new strategies are extended to the world of e-business. Implementation of Internet-related activities across industry sectors has proliferated significantly since around 1998 and the pulse will continue to grow into the foreseeable future. The analysis of Web-related data still is somewhat in an infancy stage regarding the application of high end data mining, (see Chapters 6 and 7 for the "state of the marketplace" regarding this issue). Mining methodologies that will most likely begin to be commonplace will involve such applications that relate to Web site effectiveness. One of these refers to association and sequence analysis, which refers to a statistical and algorithmic approach which identifies patterns in the activity for Web site users (see Chapter 6). In other words, this technique helps identify the direction or path with which consumers navigate through a site. This information, along with the addition of profiles connected with navigation, helps e-business managers optimize Web site design to more effectively accommodate the targeted user. The bottom line to this application however once again entails applying current mining technology in more flexible applications.

The greatest potential for value added returns and therefore the future direction of data mining most likely includes three areas:

1) Effective and timely communication of mining results to corresponding users.
2) Continued streamlining or simplification of the data access and extraction process for mining.
3) Closing the knowledge gap between high level miners and business managers/decision makers.

The first point refers to the entire realm of business intelligence and addresses the topic of diffusion of value added information. This is integral to the evolution of the information economy as email, intranets, extranets and the Internet have all enhanced the communication flow between employees within an enterprise, between firms and their partners, distributors and subsidiaries and finally from businesses to the ultimate consumer. The more people know about their business, the less room for uncertainty and inefficiencies.

Many attributes of the business intelligence spectrum (e.g. OLAP, query and reporting) initially provided a value added as many business users had access to large multidimensional cubes and a variety of reports that were available on servers, which were accessible via LANs and workstations. This software enhanced the business intelligence of those who used it, which had grown because of the LAN workstation environment.

The Wonders of Internet Related Technology

Just when companies thought things couldn't be improved upon, the evolution of the Internet and development of intranets and extranets added a new dimension to the word communication. OLAP cubes and customized reports are now made available to all conceivable users via this technology. It is this vehicle that may hold the greatest promise for data mining analysis as well.

User Friendly Mining Reports

There's no doubt that data mining often entails a high level user who has an understanding of not only sophisticated statistics but also how to arrange data in a way that best provides robust results within a given application. High end regression or neural net-based models that entail a great deal of designer/user interaction require advanced training in such areas. In fact, the results of such models are often difficult to communicate in a value added fashion to non-miners throughout an organization. This refers to the knowledge gap addressed in the last chapter. However the difficulties here are not insurmountable. Once reliable, predictive models are created, value added results need not be infiltrated with high level statistical jargon. Regression models produce beta coefficients. Neural net models produce a series of weights which measure the relationship between descriptive variables and the targeted measure. Classification and segmentation mining results produce decision tree and graphical reports of corresponding relationships between variables (segments of variables) and targeted measures. Once again, the highly complex equations, algorithms and statistical measurement techniques are not required by the every day user. Therefore, the proliferation/communication of mining results can be done in a way that benefits the consumers of this information via a network that can access the appropriate user base.

What am I referring to? Data mining models, analysis and results that are portrayed in a user friendly format that are accessible via intranets and extranets provide the highest level analytics to decision makers throughout an organization. What the user sees and accesses include:

1) Static reports and graphics that illustrate relationships between variables that affect their business.
2) Interactive reports that enable users to perform "what if" and sensitivity analysis to gain a greater understanding of how target variables change given inputs in descriptive variables.
3) Greater integration with existing reporting technology (e.g., reporting model results in OLAP cubes or standard reports).

The points mentioned above generally address the issue of enhancing the communication of value added information throughout an organization. In the BI spectrum, the lower level information that is proliferated to the greatest number of people comes in the form of functional area specific, customized reports via data extraction and report writing software. The next level includes some more complex methodology where fewer users navigate through cubes in an OLAP environment. This process entails an aspect of analysis (e.g., slicing and dicing through dimensions to answer a question) and generally results in a report form (e.g., graphic or non-graphic representation of a portion of a cube that corresponds to a particular application).

The commonality to the above procedures involves the notion of creating a report of application specific information. The highest level of the BI continuum incorporates complex quantitative data mining, which probably is broken up as 75% to 80% modeling and analysis and 20% reporting. In other words, the model creation and analysis process of mining accounts for the majority of user activity and the resulting reports play only a small part in their current state. This of course is a ballpark figure used to illustrate the much heavier weight allocated to the analytical process of mining. The key to the future of data mining is to increase the space of the reporting portion of various methodologies. The heavy-duty analytic requirements to producing reliable mining analysis will most likely remain an essential part of this analytical space. However, mining results can be significantly improved upon and proliferated to a greater number of users via effectively designed user interfaces communicated over Internet related technology (e.g., intranets and extranets) through a customized portal.

What you have then is an environment where high level and expert miners can specialize in the creation of value added models, the results of which are displayed in a business friendly format. This environment helps minimize the potential for inaccurate mining analysis that can result from dispersing complex technology to a great number of individuals that may not be qualified to create high-level quantitative, statistical models.

Static reports can include segmentation and decision tree displays such as:

- Demographic profiles of customers or business operations according to activity rates and potential activity rates for CRM applications, (B2B, B2C).
- Manufacturing process flowcharts (decision trees) that correspond to such target measures as defect rates.
- Advertising, marketing and pricing affects on performance measures (e.g. sales).
- Seasonality affects on a particular measure.
- Web site effectiveness
- Credit Profiles

Regression and Neural Network Reports

Neural network and regression models can portray elasticity coefficients and impact measures depicting the strength of the relationship between variables and the target they seek to explain. More importantly, users can access pre-built optimized models to perform what if/sensitivity analysis and forecasting. By changing one or more inputs of an existing model, users can view the corresponding changes in the output measure. This is also value-added because once models have been constructed and optimized, users would not be able to alter the underlying integrity of the model (e.g. beta coefficients in regression) but can only make changes to input variables. This is important because it maintains the integrity of the model which was created by specialists while giving the user the functionality that is important to them. Common examples of these types of reports, which can be static or interactive, may include:

- Advertising and marketing effectiveness on sales, market share or customer activity measures.
- Pricing impacts on sales.
- Customer profiles for activity rankings.
- Seasonality effects on an output measure.
- Process changes on output, defect rate or cost measures.
- Employee activity descriptors on performance or retention (HR).
- Descriptive changes (demographic) on credit measures.

The are many more applications which can be added to this list once the user considers creating a fully robust mining analysis of a given business application.

CRM One More Time

This topic of augmenting the reporting characteristic of mining analysis is particularly applicable to the world of CRM applications. The popular mining application of customer profiling identifies the particular characteristics of a given client that correspond with a particular activity rate (e.g., response to a campaign or mailing, purchases of a product or service, views or click throughs of a particular Web site or potential cross-purchasing activities).

Mining methodologies such as neural networks, regression and market basket analysis are commonly used to create models which measure the relationship between customer characteristics/descriptors and the corresponding activity rate. The key to the future of such activities once again entails the streamlining of the report mechanisms that illustrate the results of the various mining activities. For example, some software organizations have developed call center applications which utilize mining algorithms to score customers as more probable of responding to or purchasing a particular good or service as they log into Web sites or call in to call center service centers of a given enterprise. Report mechanisms then display customer information which enables customer service reps or appropriate sales personal to more effectively service a client.

The future of mining once again doesn't appear to be in the application of innovative algorithms which somehow provide a crystal ball to better facilitate CRM applications, but it lies more in the proliferation of the output that mining methodologies produce regarding client activity. CRM isn't limited to call center activities but is imbedded in every day operations of an organization. It entails not only B2C environments but B2B applications as well. Data mining results must be made available to those users whose activities correspond with the mining attributes. In other words, the more specific call center applications will most likely be expanded to enterprise wide reporting and CRM operations involving both B2B and B2C environments.

More streamlined reporting of mining results (e.g., customer activity analysis) will most likely entail a greater integration with data storage, extraction and reporting software in the current BI spectrum. Model results can be stored in a data repository that can be accessed by sequel extraction software which can be displayed in a more basic report format or in an OLAP cube environment. With the use of intranets, the reporting vehicles can quickly be dispersed to the appropriate users throughout organizations. This process has concentrated on the CRM space, however communication of mining results in the reporting mechanisms of the BI spectrum could include many, if not all of the applications mentioned in this book.

CONTINUED STREAMLINING OR SIMPLIFICATION OF THE DATA ACCESS AND EXTRACTION PROCESS FOR MINING

The next topic addresses the issue of simplifying a portion of the Mining process which involves the tedious activity of data gathering, extraction and access by miners in an acceptable format that facilitates a reliable mining analysis. This operation is not unique to the data mining space but involves the entire spectrum of data warehousing (data storage and access technology).

Core information for a given organization resides in a number of sources from vast data warehouses to a number of data marts. Software technology such as automated sequel code generating technology can provide a mechanism that simplifies the data extraction process. However, the current state of this technology still involves a number of tedious and time consuming steps that are outside the scope of mining skills, as they refer more to data warehousing skills. As was mentioned earlier in this book, once a particular mining process has been developed (e.g., variables and corresponding formats have been optimized) the mining process can become more of a routine. The element that will simplify this routine will include data extraction or access technology that is more simple to work with (e.g., can read data from multiple sources and can call variables according to particular formats and time periods). This functionality could be incorporated within mining software packages as well.

Enhancements in this area would reduce the time requirements of modeling, which results in more models in a given time and ultimately cuts down labor-intensive activities which promotes efficiency for the firm.

Enhancements in Data Storage Techniques (Warehouses and Marts)

When addressing data access and retrieval (extraction) one must first consider the process by which data is initially gathered. The evolution of the information economy has largely focused on the proliferation of information which begins with the capturing, storage and access of business related data. The quantity and quality of business related information today far exceeds that of any time in history. In reality however, the efficiency with which this data is stored and accessed is still far from optimal. The focus of large organizations continues to revolve around capturing the appropriate data in an acceptable format that is easily accessible to analyze and proliferate throughout an organization. The pitfalls of today include the inability to capture relevant data in complementary formats in some type of logical storage facility. Some obstacles that firms face today include:

1) What type of data (content and format) do we need to capture?
2) How do we determine the contents of data marts?
3) Which type of IT vendors offer the greatest integration with other systems?

It is this data warehousing issue that relates to the streamlining process for mining mentioned above. The more efficiently that data is stored, (e.g., the right data to avoid overload, in a logically related structure), the easier will be the data access and extraction process.

Extraction technology of today, which can retrieve data from multiple sources (marts) and store it in a common retainer is beginning to address this issue, but the process still must begin from the ground up and that is the collection and storage of original data.

As the process continues to evolve, it may become an integral (standard) feature in data mining technology to more easily extract mining related information. However, the bottom line remains, the more efficiently data is stored (storage facility, formats and potential commonality between variables) the greater will be the ability of future mining technologies to incorporate data access and extraction capabilities to perform mining analysis.

CLOSING THE GAP (The Evolution of the Workforce and Data Mining Technology)

The final issue regarding the future of data mining addresses the proliferation of mining analysis throughout a given enterprise in a manner different from the one mentioned above. This last issue refers to the knowledge evolution of the workforce. Over the past five years, there has no doubt been a retraining of employees at all levels of management throughout organizations across industries. This retraining involves the ability of an employee to operate and work handily with information technology. Employees today are almost required to work on PCs connected to local servers and operate a number of software related applications.

The evolution of today's employee probably began with the ability to work with spreadsheets and word processing software. This has progressed to performing more complex spreadsheet related activities, proficiency with email functionality and working with other software systems. For example, the proliferation of business intelligence software has brought many into the OLAP realm of multidimensional cube navigation and graphic analysis.

The Step Up to Mining

The step up to mining will probably involve a convergence of two areas:
1) The continued simplification of statistical testing of mining methodologies and results and imbedded optimization processes which provide more business friendly solutions.
2) The increased knowledge of the worker in understanding mining methodologies.

Over the past years, mining procedures have continually evolved towards greater user friendliness which has increased its appeal to the business user. The functionality of data retrieval, manipulation and modeling have been simplified and much of the complex statistical terminology has been transformed in a way that it maintains its mathematical integrity but is easier to comprehend to the business user. On the other hand, as data mining plays more of an integral part in the analytical procedures of decision makers, the retraining towards a better knowledge of statistics of decision makers will most likely grow. Knowledge of terminology such as R^2, t-tests, correlations will become more commonplace in the decision makers environment. Today's proliferation of "6 Sigma" techniques (see Chapter 3) across industry sectors is a prime example.

The simplification of mining methods may involve the addition of peripheral quantitative techniques which would provide solutions to specific answers in a more business friendly environment. Regression and neural network models enable users to perform "what if" analysis for a given application (e.g., how does my demand change if I change my price?). Many times business analysts seek to identify optimal levels of parameters (driving variables) for a particular application. For example, at what level of advertising, price and promotion do I achieve the greatest revenue?

Technology such as linear programming that performs max/min computations for corresponding variables helps answer the optimization question (Lee, 1985). In other words, I know how my variables interact but what are the optimal levels of these driving variables that produce the best result? Although some mining technologies have incorporated this functionality, the future will most likely involve the proliferation of this methodology as a common offering among mining vendors. This final topic helps bridge the knowledge gap between mining models and business users, as the mining process becomes more business/user friendly.

A Narrower Gap and Increased Business Knowledge

The convergence of these areas, higher statistical skills of workers and simplified mining functionality, will result in a narrowing of the knowledge gap between high level miners and the average business analyst. This convergence should result in the more widespread implementation of mining methodology throughout functional areas in firms across industries. Will the gap between miners and general business analysts ever be closed? I would venture to say, not for a long time. This assumption delves into the space of specialization of labor. High level miners will fill that space in the world of commerce, as this activity generally requires a high and unique skill level. But this is not to say that middle level managers will continue to be perplexed by "rocket science" jargon that is often a part of the mining process. The gap should narrow which may ultimately result in a greater number of individuals who can perform some level of mining applications throughout a given organization or at least understand what mining reports mean to their world.

The final result then is a progression not only of making complex technology more user friendly but also raising the knowledge level of the average worker and decision maker. The future should entail an environment where data access and extraction of appropriate information in usable formats is less cumbersome and time consuming for the mining process. Most importantly, the output of mining analysis should become more available in an understandable format to the decision making population and finally, as stated above, the progress will not be limited to augmenting the technology side of things but the knowledge level of the average worker as well. As a result, mining methodologies and output should become more comprehendible to a greater number of workers throughout an organization (Tapscott, 1999).

CONCLUSION

Up until the middle to end of the 1990s, many had been skeptical as to the impact information technology has had on the world of commerce. However, by the turn of the century, there appears to be little question as to the efficiency enhancing power state of the art IT has provided organizations across industries.

The evolution of computer processing power, software, telecommunications and Internet related technology (intranets and extranets) have come together to form a cohesive, complementary space that facilitates the storage, retrieval, manipulation, analysis and communication of vast amounts of information. This has provided reliable, understandable and value added information to employees at all levels which has reduced the uncertainty of conducting business in all parts of an enterprise.

Data mining and business intelligence plays an integral role in the knowledge enhancing process by providing the means to transform data into information. The evolution of the information age is still in an infancy stage. Issues such as the proliferation of information technology around the globe along with the introduction and implementation of new technologies (wireless communication and complementary applications as was mentioned in Chapter 6), should provide new and interesting applications in the world of business intelligence. Continuous innovations in technology and enhanced labor skills will no doubt continue to improve the process in which organizations operate, domestically and around the globe. As a result, firms should continue to increase the efficiency with which they provide goods and services that more accurately meet the needs of corresponding consumers. The results of which should benefit both producers and consumers. There is no doubt we are living in interesting times.

REFERENCES

Lee, S., Moore, D. and Taylor, E. (1985). *Management Science* 3rd Edition, Allyn and Bacon Publishing.

Tapscott, Don (1999). Creating *Value in the Network Economy,* Harvard Business School Press, Boston.

Appendix (1)

Accepted economic theory, which addresses the topic of business efficiency or productivity, can incorporate the following functional forms.

COST MINIMIZATION

The first equation involves the minimization of a standard cost function where:

Given the simple production function:

$$Q^t = f(x^t, t) + \text{error}$$

where:

Q^t **output is produced during time (t) and the input set used during period (t), $x^t = (x^t_1, x^t_2, x^t_N)$**

Then:

$$C(Q_t, p_t, t) = \min_x \{p_t x: f(x,t) \bullet Q_t, x \bullet O_N)$$

In the above function, a producer faces a positive vector of input prices (pt = $(p^t_1, p^t_2, \ldots p^t_N) > O_N$ where O_N is a null vector 1*N dimension during period (t) and seeks to minimize costs in a competitive market.

MORE COMPLEX PRODUCTION FUNCTIONS

To estimate the returns to factors of production or inputs to a given production process, standard economic theory involves the incorporation of more complex production functions. One such form, the Cobb Douglas, enables the estimation of factor input elasticity coefficients and is depicted below.

$$Q = (IL^B, I^B, IK^B, K^B)$$

Where: Q is output for a firm and

IL is the input of Information Technology Labor
L   is the input of Non-IT Labor
IK is IT capital
K   is Non IT capital

(B) values are variables that denote the elasticity of each of the input factors.

To estimate the function one only needs to linearize the form, which yields:

$$\ln(Q) = B1\ln(IL) + B2\ln(L) + B3\ln(IK) + B4\ln(K)$$

B1 through B4 reflect the percent change in output given a 1% change in the given input.

APPENDIX (2)

MARKET BASKET ANALYSIS
History

Market Basket Analysis (MBA) is the practice of finding out what products customers typically buy together. This knowledge is valuable:

- In retail outlets, it can aid store layouts. "Impulse buy" products can be placed next to "regular buy" products with which they are associated. "Regular buy" products can be place some distance from associated "regular buy" products, encouraging the customer to tour the entire store.
- Cross-promotional opportunities can be identified. In retail environments, special offers can be made to encourage product purchasers to buy associated products. In other industries, MBA can be used to identify which customers would be the best focus of marketing campaigns.
- "Cause and effect" relationships can be identified, making it possible to predict what a customer is likely to buy next.

Until recently, MBA was only justified in the largest of companies due to the effort of collecting the data. This has changed dramatically for two reasons:

- Barcode scan data automatically records the required information and can exploit it in real time at the cash register in the form of targeted promotions printed on the purchaser's receipt.
- Web sites automatically record purchase data and can exploit it by immediately presenting the surfing customer with targeted product recommendations. A classic example of this is *Amazon.com*'s web-site. As the customer looks at the description of a product, a paragraph is added which says, "People who bought this product also bought..."

MBA is achieved by analyzing sales transaction data. Additional factors, such as region, channel, day of week (or time of year) and demographic factors about the customer can enrich the analysis.

MARKET BASKET ANALYSIS IN PRACTICE

MBA is usually implemented in-house rather than with off-the-shelf software. Since this is the case, this discussion will include a simple example. Any reader wishing to implement MBA can test their system with these numbers.

The sample data considers six products bought in twenty transactions:

Transn.	Quantity Bought					
	Juice	Tea	Coffee	Milk	Sugar	Pop
1	0	0	0	0	0	0
2	0	2	2	4	3	0
3	1	0	0	0	0	0
4	0	1	0	0	0	0
5	1	2	1	1	0	0
6	0	2	1	3	2	0
7	0	0	0	0	0	6
8	0	0	0	0	0	0
9	4	0	0	0	0	0
10	0	0	1	1	0	0
11	0	0	0	0	0	6
12	0	0	1	1	0	0
13	0	0	0	0	0	5
14	0	0	0	0	0	0
15	1	2	0	2	0	0
16	0	1	1	1	2	1
17	1	0	1	0	0	0
18	2	0	0	0	0	0
19	0	0	0	0	0	2
20	3	0	0	0	0	3

MBA looks at transactions to see which products get bought together. To do this, the transactions are analyzed to calculate:

N, the total number of orders.

n_i, the number of orders in which product i is bought.

x_{ij}, the number of orders in which both products i and j are bought.

In the case of this example, N is 20. n_i and x_{ij} are therefore:

	Juice	Tea	Coffee	Milk	Sugar	Pop
Ni	7	6	7	7	3	6

Xij	Juice	Tea	Coffee	Milk	Sugar	Pop
Juice	7	2	2	2	0	1
Tea	2	6	4	5	3	1
Coffee	2	4	7	6	3	1
Milk	2	5	6	7	3	1
Sugar	0	3	3	3	3	1
Pop	1	1	1	1	1	6

From this data, four measures of product association can be calculated: support, confidence, improvement and value.

Support

$$S_{ij} = \frac{x_{ij}}{N} \times 100\%$$

Support	Juice	Tea	Coffee	Milk	Sugar	Pop
Juice		10%	10%	10%	0%	5%
Tea	10%		20%	25%	15%	5%
Coffee	10%	20%		30%	15%	5%
Milk	10%	25%	30%		15%	5%
Sugar	0%	15%	15%	15%		5%
Pop	5%	5%	5%	5%	5%	

Note that the leading diagonal values, which would always be 100%, are meaningless and have been omitted. Also note that the table is symmetric across the diagonal. For reporting purposes, this information is often best left as a table, but for comparison with the other measures, let us show it as a chart:

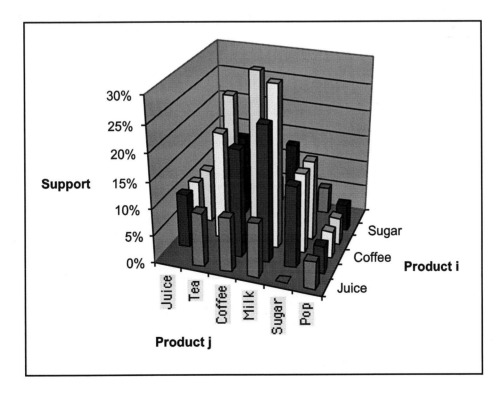

Confidence

Confidence $C_{i \to j}$ measures the percentage of buyers of product i who also buy product j and is calculated as:

$$C_{i \to j} = \frac{x_{ij}}{n_i} \times 100\%$$

For the data in the example, this gives:

		Product j					
		Juice	Tea	Coffee	Milk	Sugar	Pop
Product i	Juice		33%	29%	29%	0%	17%
	Tea	29%		57%	71%	100%	17%
	Coffee	29%	67%		86%	100%	17%
	Milk	29%	83%	86%		100%	17%
	Sugar	0%	50%	43%	43%		17%
	Pop	14%	17%	14%	14%	33%	

Note that the table is not symmetric across the diagonal: the average Sugar buyer is twice as likely to buy Pop as vice versa. For web-site cross-selling, the confidence measure can be used to inform the site visitor of other products they might be interested in. For purposes of comparison, the confidence data is graphically depicted as follows:

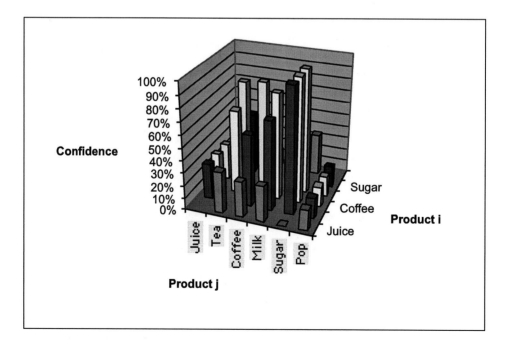

Improvement

Improvement I_{ij} measures how much more likely product i buyers are to buy product j than customers in general:

$$I_{ij} = \frac{N \cdot x_{ij}}{n_i \cdot n_j}$$

For the data in the example, this gives:

Improvement	Juice	Tea	Coffee	Milk	Sugar	Pop
Juice	0.95	0.82	0.82	0.00	0.48	
Tea	0.95		1.90	2.38	3.33	0.56
Coffee	0.82	1.90		2.45	2.86	0.48
Milk	0.82	2.38	2.45		2.86	0.48
Sugar	0.00	3.33	2.86	2.86		1.11
Pop	0.48	0.56	0.48	0.48	1.11	

Surprisingly, this table is symmetric across the diagonal. This measure is commonly used to identify cross-selling promotional opportunities. It identifies which promotion is most likely to appear to the customer. For example, a sugar buyer is nearly three times as likely to want milk than the average customer. For purposes of comparison, the improvement data is graphically depicted as follows:

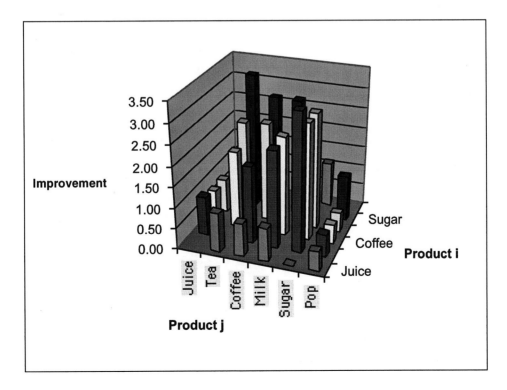

Value

Value is a similar measure to improvement except that it measures the cross-selling potential in dollars profit rather than simple unit sales:

$$V_{i \rightarrow j} = m_j \times I_{ij}$$

For the data in the example, this gives:

Value	Juice	Tea	Coffee	Milk	Sugar	Pop
Juice		10	15	2	0	10
Tea	29		34	5	13	11
Coffee	24	19		5	11	10
Milk	24	24	44		11	10
Sugar	0	33	51	6		22
Pop	14	6	9	1	4	

Because the margins of the promoted products have been incorporated, the table is no longer symmetric across the diagonal. This measure identifies the most profitable cross-selling opportunities. For example, promoting sugar to coffee buyers has the highest value payoff. This measure can be used to generate targeted discount coupons. Incorporating the margin information directs us clearly to the most profitable opportunities, as the chart shows:

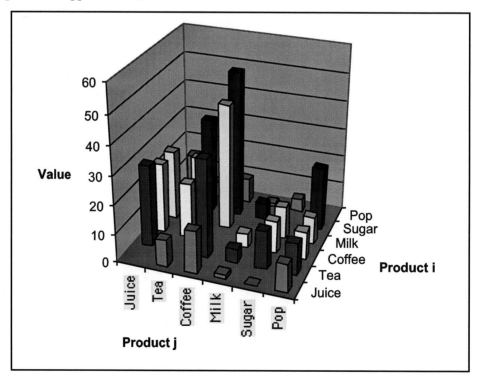

Note the difference between the improvement and value measures: sugar and milk are low margin, and so the value measure does not attempt to cross sell them even though an attempt to cross-sell would probably be successful.

BEYOND BASIC MBA

There are many ways to extend this analysis, depending on the products being sold:

- Look for links between three or more products. This is useful for identifying product bundles, such as popular mixes of ingredients in a sandwich. In practice, this approach increases calculation times exponentially and has limited payoff.
- Take account of the quantity of product ordered in each purchase.
- Segment the analysis by region, channel, day of week (or time of year) or demographic factors about the customer, etc.
- If customer identity is recorded in the transaction detail, the analysis can be used to link products bought in this order with products bought in subsequent transactions.

Market Basket Analysis is discussed further in Berry (1997).

Appendix (3)

Econometric modeling entails the utilization of statistical inference testing. Some of the more popular statistical tests include:

Coefficient of Determination (R²): A statistical measure of how good the estimated regression equation is; designated as R^2 (read as R-Squared). Simply put, it is a measure of "goodness of fit" in the regression. Therefore, the higher the R-Square, the more confidence we can have in our equation.

$$R2 = 1 - \frac{\Sigma(Y - Y')^2}{\Sigma(Y - Y_{avg})^2}$$

where Y = the observed value of the dependent variable
Y' = the estimated value based on the equation.

T-Statistic: A measure of the statistical significance of an independent variable in explaining the dependent variable Y. It is determined by dividing the estimated regression coefficient (b) by its standard error.

F-Statistic: (F-Test): In statistics the ratio of two mean squares (variances) often can be used to test the significance of some item of interest. For example, in regression, the ratio of (mean square due to the regression) to (mean square due to error) can be used to test the overall significance of the regression model. By looking up F-Tables, the degree of significance of the computed F-value can be determined. Simply stated, the F-Statistic measures the variance explained by the model to the variance of that not explained by the model or the residual.

Regression Coefficients or Beta Values: When a dependent measure Y is regressed against a set of independent measures X_1 through X_k the analyst wishes to estimate the values of the unknown coefficients by least squares procedures. For example, in a linear regression equation Y = a + bX, (a) and (b) are regression coefficients. Specifically (a) is called the y-intercept or constant, while (b) is called a slope. The properties of these regression coefficients can be used to understand the importance of each independent variable (as it relates to Y) and the interrelatedness among the independent variables (as they relate to Y).

Durbin Watson Statistic: A summary measure of the amount of autocorrelation in the error terms of the regression. By comparing the computed value of the Durbin Watson test with the appropriate values from the table of values of the DW Statistic, the significance can be determined. This statistic helps determine whether the residual terms are independent of each other.

Definitions taken from "Strategic Business Forecasting," Shim, Siegel & Liew

Appendix (4)

What is Six Sigma?

What is Six Sigma (both a simple and a complex question)?

In mathematical terms, six sigma is a statistically derived performance target for operating with only 3.4 defects per million (i.e., a target in which a process performs in such a way that the control limits are six standard deviations apart relative to the mean output). In contrast, three sigma reflects operations with as many as 66,800 defects per million.

The *Six Sigma Quality Management System* (Six Sigma) is a systematic approach for improving the quality of manufacturing and organizational-work processes. Six Sigma starts with the customer to clearly define process demand, and then links ambitious process-improvement goals with a set of quantitative metrics and statistical tools. Six Sigma was originally developed at Motorola in the 1980s and then adopted by GE and Allied Signal in the mid-1990s prior to its wide-spread corporate acceptance during the past two years. Six Sigma is all about creating a constancy of purpose toward the improvement of quality and productivity of a process (Deming). Six Sigma is being applied as much to marketing, service, financial and sales work processes as it is being applied to engineering and manufacturing processes.

Six Sigma is the rigorous implementation of an array of proven quality principles and statistical techniques that have been best practices for the past two decades. It is a highly quantitative and analytical approach to continuous improvement with the disciplined use of facts, data and statistical analysis, and the diligent attention to managing and improving processes. Six Sigma provides a perspective on the variance of a process to fully understand the "real" performance (no longer hiding behind the averages). Six Sigma helps an organization focus on defect prevention, cycle time reduction and eliminating non-value added activities.

Quality – what is it in a Six Sigma world?

At the heart of Six Sigma is the notion that quality saves money. Quality in the Six Sigma system is a measure of how well your customer's needs are being met, not merely meeting internal specifications. The sigma value is a quality metric that indicates how well a process is performing. Six Sigma is not a quality assurance plan but a work-process control strategy.

Sigma Value	Process Yield*	Defects per Million*
1.0	30.9%	690,000
2.0	69.2%	308,000
3.0	93.3%	66,800
4.0	99.4%	6,210
5.0	99.98%	320
6.0	99.999%	3.4

*assuming the mean output of a process may drift up to 1.5 sigma from the target output.

Why use Six Sigma?

Incorporation of Six Sigma into our performance management systems will establish the following business priorities:
- greater focus on the customer
- data-driven work-process management
- focus towards process efficiency and improvement
- well informed, proactive decision making
- improve collaboration across business units

The benefits from successful implementation of Six Sigma include:
- increased efficiency and higher profit margins
- timely execution of strategic change
- further enhanced value to customers
- sustained success for continuous improvement programs
- common goals and consistent metrics throughout the organization.

How is Six Sigma applied?

The systematic approach to executing a Six Sigma project includes five steps:
1. *define* the expectations for the process
2. *measure* the quality attributes for the process
3. *analyze* when and where defects occur
4. *improve* the process to obtain the desired quality
5. *control* the process to sustain the new level of performance

*The above material taken from the following: GEpower.com, honeywell.com, DOW.com, www.qa_inc.com <http://www.qa_inc.com> (*The Complete Guide to Six Sigma *by Thomas Pyzdek), www.bestpracticedatabase.com <http://www.bestpracticedatabase.com>, and* Six Sigma: The Breakthrough Strategy *by M. Harry and R. Schroeder.*

SIX SIGMA AND DATA MINING

The Six Sigma methodology entails the application of statistical techniques, which are used to identify the relationships between variables that underpin a given process. These statistical techniques can include:

- Chi-Square tests
- t-tests
- Analysis of Variance tests
- Multivariate Analytical tests

Data mining methodologies such as segmentation, regression and to some extent neural network methodologies incorporate many of the statistical techniques above. Hence the connection of 6 Sigma to data mining.

In a regression application:

The various forms of regression analysis concentrate on using existing data to predict future results. The most common is "Linear Regression" (or simple regression), which is used for two variables. This can be illustrated by using a copier example:

Percy's Copy Repair Shop wants to show clients the value of its maintenance service contract. Having gathered data on the relationships between Time Maintenance and Copy Defects, they found that defect rates tend to increase by 15 percent for every two-week period without maintenance. Using the tool of Linear Regression, they were able to predict to a prospective customer that by the third month after their last "emergency" service call, they'd be getting about 25% "defective" copies. The prediction turned out to be pretty accurate, and now the customer has a bi-weekly service agreement with Percy's.

Multiple Regression, like Multivariate analysis, examines the relationship among several factors and the results. In a process environment, examples could include all those shown in the following table.

Using Multiple Regression, you would be able to quantify the impact of each of these X's on the Y's – and to see how they interact. In more advanced applications,

Multiple Regression is applied to create models to predict the results when combinations of factors interact under various conditions.

Table I.

Process	Unit or Item	X1 (Input variable)	X2 (Process variable)	X3 (Process variable)	Y (Output or result variable)
Software Installation	Software Package	Size of Software (MB)	Number of Users On Network	Server Processor Speed (MHz)	System Downtime during Install (Minutes)
Hotel Reservation and Check-In	Reservation	Hold Time to talk to Reservation Agent (seconds)	Number of days reserved	Number of Agents on duty in Call Center	Time to check in a guest (minutes)

Above material taken from "Six Sigma Way," Pande, 336, 367.

As was mentioned in this work, neural network data mining techniques are also suitable for the above analysis.

ABOUT THE AUTHORS

Stephan Kudyba began his career in the investment banking industry where he spent over a decade of his life analyzing the state of the global economy. His experience has included such activities as international economist/market analyst and risk exposure management, which involved the creation of sophisticated models that identified trends in securities prices. Over the years, he has worked in such institutions as Citibank (New York), Dresdner Bank (Frankfurt, Germany and New York) during which he obtained a Masters in Business Administration with a finance concentration.

In order to fully grasp the changing nature of economic activity as a result of the evolving information age, Dr. Kudyba obtained a PhD in economics at Rensselaer Polytechnic Institute with a special focus on information technology and firm level productivity. He is now an economic consultant with Cognos Corporation where he applies data mining and business intelligence technology to devise productivity enhancing strategies for organizations around the globe. He also has combined his knowledge of the information economy with his investments experience and provides in-depth analysis of global investment markets, which is available on his Web Site www.marketdr.net. Dr. Kudyba can be contacted at marketdoctor@marketdr.net.

Richard Hoptroff obtained a PhD in Physics in London for developing optimization algorithms and neural networks for industrial applications including control systems and robot vision. After graduating in 1992, he applied the same techniques to economics and business modeling. After initially working as a consultant, he started Right Information Systems (RIS), a software company dedicated to producing what was to become known as data mining software. RIS's premier product was 4Thought, a neural-network based modeling and forecasting package. In 1997, RIS was acquired by Cognos Inc of Ottawa, Canada, where he became Director of Data Mining. In 1999 he returned to independent consulting and is currently based in Amsterdam in the Netherlands.

INDEX